I didn't know what to expect when I first began reading Jenny Randle's book *Getting to Know God's Voice*. To say I was more than pleasantly surprised is a massive understatement. If you hunger to hear the voice of the Spirit and grow deeper in your intimacy with Jesus, this exceptionally well-crafted interactive journey is an excellent place to start. Trust me, you will be greatly blessed!

Sam Storms
author of *Practicing the Power*
member of the Council of The Gospel Coalition
pastor, Bridgeway Church, Oklahoma City

Some people speak from encouragement, and some from experience. Jenny is one of the few who speak effortlessly from both. *Getting to Know God's Voice* will have you feeling encouraged to encounter a deeper understanding and walk with the Spirit of God. The message in these pages is timeless and necessary for anyone who seeks to not just know about God, but encounter Him daily.

Candace Payne
author, speaker, podcaster, viral sensation

Getting to Know God's Voice tackles this topic with the serious, gospel-centered approach it demands. It will stir you to open your heart and ears to God in a fresh way.

Mark Schilling
pastor, Redeemer Church, Rome, New York

Jenny has a way of creatively introducing the most misunderstood person of the Trinity—the Holy Spirit. What makes this message so powerful is that she does it in a way that shares biblical truth while creating space for you to experience God in the daily moments of life. As you read, you'll find not only freedom but also a firm foundation for your faith as you're getting to know God's voice. Thank you, Jenny, for reminding us that God is speaking and that we get to respond!

Alli Worthington
author of *Fierce Faith* and *Breaking Busy*

D1474513

Some books strengthen your spirit; others develop your mind. In *Getting to Know God's Voice*, Jenny does both. You are about to embrace one of the most life-changing and powerful gifts—the Holy Spirit. This is a must-have book for anyone looking to experience God's presence.

Roma Downey

Emmy® nominated actress, producer, and *New York Times* bestselling author

Thank you, Jenny, for creating a complete sensory experience at the point of divine access. A way for us to enter into the heavenlies. A way for us to know the mind of Christ and step into the supernatural realm with Him, where life is truly lived. I couldn't love and recommend this book more! Within 31 days of reading, the mind of your heart will awaken to desires you once thought deafened, numb, or lost forever. Jenny, thank you for carving out a path to the voice of God. I will read this book over and over again.

Kasey Van Norman

professional counselor, bestselling author, Bible teacher

God has always wanted to be close to us—to talk to, encourage, comfort, lead, and love us. And there is no one who wants to help us know Him and His voice more than Jenny Randle! She is a friend we can trust who will not just tell us but actually show us how to recognize God's voice so we can experience His presence and power in our everyday lives. My only regret is that younger me didn't have this resource when I was trying to figure it all out on my own.

Renee Swope

bestselling author of *A Confident Heart*

GETTING TO
KNOW
GOD'S
VOICE

JENNY RANDLE

HARVEST HOUSE PUBLISHERS
EUGENE, OREGON

To Matt,
who champions our family and created
space for these words to breathe.
I love you.

Cover and interior design by Juicebox Designs

Getting to Know God's Voice
Copyright © 2020 by Jenny Randle
Published by Harvest House Publishers
Eugene, Oregon 97408
www.harvesthousepublishers.com

ISBN 978-0-7369-8117-0 (pbk.)
ISBN 978-0-7369-8118-7 (eBook)

Library of Congress Control Number: 2020941237

Printed in the United States of America

20 21 22 23 24 25 26 27 28 / VP / 10 9 8 7 6 5 4 3 2 1

WHEN YOU GET TO KNOW GOD'S VOICE, EVERYTHING CHANGES.

CONTENTS

A NOTE FROM JENNY

To the ones whose hearts burn for Jesus,

Jesus came into my life in high school when I attended a small-town church. That's where He became real to me, and for the first time, I experienced the power of Holy Spirit (who is so personal, I drop the "the" before His name). *Everything changed.* God used that church to establish and strengthen my relationship with Him.

As I have matured in the faith, I've worked to develop a biblical understanding of Triune God and explored the role I get to play by using the giftings on my life. I've also prayerfully wrestled with an important question for more than a decade: What do a Christian person and a local church community look like when they have a healthy theology of Holy Spirit?

Oh my, have I seen unhealthy demonstrations in church communities and individuals (including me). I've run with Catholics and Protestants, theological conservatives and liberals, evangelicals and charismatics and mystics, cessationists and continuationists. I've been on the receiving end of prayer from ministers who physically manipulated and pushed people down so they appeared to have been hit with the power of God. I've also seen ministers avoid pressing into the move of God and miss out on what seemed like divine opportunities.

Maybe you've experienced those extremes too. If so, perhaps you'll agree that it's time to have an open and honest conversation about what it looks like to embrace Holy Spirit authentically, fully, and biblically.

Sometimes in our personal prayer times, we have acted like toddler Christians throwing tantrums because God didn't move the way we thought He should. There are other times we inadvertently worship the gifts more than the Gift-giver. We sometimes manipulate the Bible to fit our consumeristic Christianity, plead for fire to fall from heaven when it's already burning within, or neglect spiritual warfare altogether. These problems have not only harmed the church but also

and more

broken hearts, muffled our ears to hear God's voice, and blinded our eyes to what God is already doing. A theology that ghosts the Holy Ghost, or one that requires Him to perform according to our expectations, is inadequate and will do more harm than good.

Take a deep breath.

Exhale.

We are leaders, and we know how to follow Jesus. We're men and women strong in our faith, and we *get* to do better. We have to commit to try.

It's time to stop ghosting the Holy Ghost! Being led by Holy Spirit is not abnormal; it should be your normal. On the other hand, it's not mundane but miraculous. Holy Spirit is not just a onetime gift but also a relationship you *get* to partake in. He brings so much hope, even in the way we practice Christianity. Because you're a believer, Holy Spirit is indwelling in you and ministering through you so you will look more and more like Jesus.

The goal of *Getting to Know God's Voice* is to create a safe space that facilitates prayerful reflection and action in your personal life as you apply the things you're learning. Compare what you read in this book to the Holy Bible, and remember that Jesus is the solution to our brokenness—not me, you, your pastor, or even healthy theology. Jesus is making the church and its people beautiful. Let's press into Him and see how God moves. He can set communities, cities, and countries ablaze for Him as He ignites our passion. It's time to become fully alive as we hear God's voice and discover Holy Spirit in our everyday lives.

You're designed for this,

Jenny Randle

WHAT IS GETTING TO KNOW GOD'S VOICE?

It's a 31-day interactive journey that strengthens your faith and equips you to live a Spirit-led life. You'll explore different ways God can speak, experience freedom from the things that may be hindering you, and discover how to respond to the move of Holy Spirit. At the end of every lesson, a hearing aid challenge will equip you to apply what you're learning as you're getting to know God's voice.

As we build a biblical foundation, I'll share personal experiences so you can read about real-life examples. Some of these moments may seem radical and others simple, but they are all important. God's simple, quiet whispers and His roof-shattering revelations all show that He is moving, and they all matter. Keep this in mind during your own faith journey throughout this book.

Things You'll Need

- O relationship with Jesus
- O Bible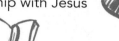
- O journal
- O pen or pencil
- O willingness to commit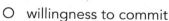
- O awesomeness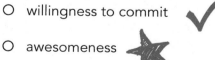
- O participation in a healthy local church
- O a spirit to do hard things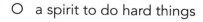

Guidelines as You Get to Know God's Voice

① This book includes a short lesson and challenge each day. The challenges, or "hearing aids," will strengthen your listening muscles as you actively participate. Some include journal prompts for further reflection. Check off the box on the contents page after you complete each chapter.

② As you work through the hearing aids, remember that the Bible is God's truth, so your feelings don't define your theology. For example, just because you can't feel God's presence doesn't mean He isn't there. Also, our supernatural experiences should coincide with biblical truth.

③ This is an interactive experience. Take greater risks as you get to know God's voice. If a hearing aid invites you to talk to a friend or stranger, pray for boldness and then go for it! You can always say, "Jenny made me do it." Or even better, "I'm practicing hearing God's voice. Can I share with you what I think He's saying?"

④ Be safe, not squirrelly or careless. As you start learning how God speaks, refrain from declaring, "Thus says the Lord" unless you're quoting Scripture in the proper context.

⑤ Remain humble. As you get to know God's voice, you may make mistakes (we all do). Repentance and verbal apologies are great if needed.

⑥ Have fun! Invite a friend on this journey with you, and use **#GettingToKnow GodsVoice** so we can get social and cheer you on in your journey. Everything is better with friends!

Commitment Contract

There's power in community and asking a friend for help. Text or call a trusted friend and ask him or her to hold you accountable to finish this book. Better yet, buy the person a copy and do it together!

I, _____, commit to discovering Holy Spirit in my everyday life over the next 31 days. I'm willing to get uncomfortable, follow the guidelines, and work through the hearing aids daily as I get to know God's voice. I'm trusting Jesus to work in and through me throughout this process. May I glorify and honor Him as I do.

My accountability partner is _____.

This person committed to encouraging me to do hard things.

_____   _____
your signature   *date*

_____   _____
accountability partner signature   *date*

The "Check Yourself Before You Wreck Yourself" Test for Life's Biggest Decisions

You don't need to work through the checklist below every time God's still, small voice prompts you to do the things He wants us to do all the time, like humbly serve other people and encourage them in their everyday lives. But these seven questions will help you make life's big decisions, like *Should I move?* or *Where should I go to college?* or *Should I marry this person?* We'll look more closely at these ideas throughout the book.

1. Does what I am considering agree with Scripture?

2. Will this situation bring me closer to God?

3. What do my spiritual leaders think about this situation?

4. What is the still, small voice of God saying to me?

5. What circumstances are surrounding this situation?

6. What do my trusted friends and family say about this?

7. What response will bring peace?

AS CHRIST-FOLLOWERS,
WE HAVE HOLY SPIRIT,
WHO SPEAKS, GUIDES,
AND HELPS US POWERFULLY
STEP IN SYNC WITH HIS
WILL FOR OUR LIVES.

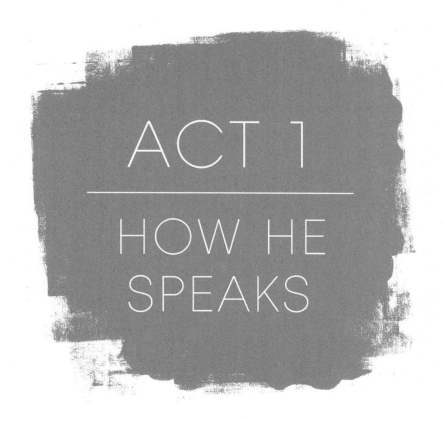

ACT 1

HOW HE SPEAKS

Lord, may we be still enough to hear the whisper

yet stirred enough to embrace the roar.

1

INTRODUCTION TO ACT 1

Stay clear of silly stories that get dressed up as religion. Exercise daily in God—no spiritual flabbiness, please! Workouts in the gymnasium are useful, but a disciplined life in God is far more so, making you fit both today and forever. You can count on this. Take it to heart. This is why we've thrown ourselves into this venture so totally. We're banking on the living God, Savior of all men and women, especially believers.

1 TIMOTHY 4:7-10 MSG

"Thanks for this gift, Dad!"

My parents gifted me an all-access gym membership, and everything changed for me in that moment. When I was feeling overwhelmed, I'd go to the gym. When my kids needed to learn to swim, we went to the gym. When I needed some clarity, I'd go to the gym and work out while listening to worship music through my headphones. For a girl to reject donuts for dumbbells was a pretty miraculous thing, and over time I was transformed. ←—*Into a gym rat.*

My gym membership came with added perks, like coaching to make me stronger, nutrition counseling if I sought it, a hot sauna to cleanse the poisonous toxins from my body, and unlimited coffee in the lobby to add some extra pep to my step. My membership granted full access not just to an area to go lift weights and build muscle but to a new lifestyle altogether.

The crazy thing is, the gym had always been there, working in the lives of people whether I acknowledged it or not. As soon as I received that all-access pass, my eyes were opened.

You can start hollering, "Preach it, sista-friend!" as I full-circle this moment. The gym is an illustration of Holy Spirit's role in your life.[1]

The moment you receive Christ as your Savior, you obtain all access. Holy Spirit indwells you, and your body becomes a temple of God.[2] You can't be a Christian apart from Holy Spirit. As we live by faith and die to self daily, Holy Spirit fills us up. We're no longer enslaved, but empowered to walk in newness of life.[3] Now that we are Christ-followers, Holy Spirit sanctifies us, strengthens us, speaks to us, guides us, and helps us powerfully step in sync with His will for our lives.

God speaks through Holy Spirit. Few people hear the audible voice of God or have a conversation with a burning bush like Moses did. Of course, God is miraculous and all-powerful, and if He wants to talk to you out loud, He can. But Holy Spirit usually moves supernaturally in ways that seem so ordinary that they get overlooked—until months or maybe decades later when we finally sneak a peek behind us to see God's puzzle pieces perfectly interconnected in a divine masterpiece. Wouldn't it be better if we didn't have to look behind us to see God's hand moving us forward?

Working in You

Knowing God's voice starts with understanding that Holy Spirit is in your life in a personal way. He is more than an "it," or a dove bumper sticker, or the last mention in the Trinity. Holy Spirit is coequal and coeternal with Father God and Jesus Christ. Learning to recognize and respond to His voice is a foundational element of Christianity.

Check out Romans 8:11 and John 14:16-17 to dig in more.

The gym empowered me to develop healthy habits and strengthened my character and attitude. The change in my life was a direct reflection of the gym. Because you are a child of God, the same Spirit who raised Christ from the dead dwells with you and in you. We *get* to answer Holy Spirit's promptings, which produce change in our lives by directing us toward repentance, righteousness, joy, purpose, and so much more.

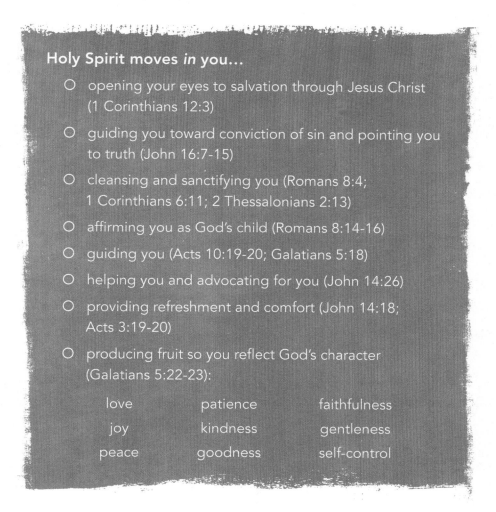

Holy Spirit moves *in* you...

O   opening your eyes to salvation through Jesus Christ (1 Corinthians 12:3)

O   guiding you toward conviction of sin and pointing you to truth (John 16:7-15)

O   cleansing and sanctifying you (Romans 8:4; 1 Corinthians 6:11; 2 Thessalonians 2:13)

O   affirming you as God's child (Romans 8:14-16)

O   guiding you (Acts 10:19-20; Galatians 5:18)

O   helping you and advocating for you (John 14:26)

O   providing refreshment and comfort (John 14:18; Acts 3:19-20)

O   producing fruit so you reflect God's character (Galatians 5:22-23):

love	patience	faithfulness
joy	kindness	gentleness
peace	goodness	self-control

Working Through You

After I'd used my gym membership a few times, I discovered that it included more than I'd originally realized. I heard about power workout classes for extra strengthening, and I saw encouraging sticky notes left on lockers. The gym also informed parents about the drug epidemic the youths in our community are facing. This gym was *so* much more than just a way to get a hot bod and feel great. It was working through its members, changing the landscape of our city and empowering generations to come.

Because you are a member of God's kingdom, Holy Spirit is working through you in a similar way. When you read through the Gospels and the book of Acts, you can see what I mean. God is actively and powerfully bringing heaven to earth in miraculous ways, and He's inviting us to join Holy Spirit as He does.

In Mark 1:8, John is preaching to a crowd and says, "I have baptized you with water, but he will baptize you with the Holy Spirit." This passage is referring to the baptism of the Holy Spirit—a confusing topic for a lot of Christians.

Since the moment you became a Christian, the presence of God has always dwelled *fully* in you. Scripture doesn't clearly say when the baptism of the Holy Spirit happens (see Acts 2 and Acts 8:14-17), but we can conclude this: The baptism of the Holy Spirit occurs in a specific moment, and that's when the empowering of Holy Spirit becomes a reality in your life. It's a defining moment that shapes your life by actively immersing you in Holy Spirit.

For some people, the baptism of the Holy Spirit occurs at the moment of salvation. For others, it happens when they become aware of the power of Holy Spirit for the first time and yield to His presence. As a result, they may exercise a spiritual gift like the ones listed on the next page. The baptism of the Holy Spirit can occur in the quietness of solitude, at a church service, or when Christians simply pray for one another.

When this happens to you, you feel the weight, power, and presence of God. You sense that His power is *in you* and cooperate as He moves *through you*. The baptism of the Holy Spirit includes a significant shift in your perspective—you acknowledge Holy Spirit's power in your life for the first time. What changed? It wasn't His power; it was your perspective.

And then throughout our Christian walk, we experience the filling of Holy

Spirit repeatedly as we yield and submit control to Him. We're embracing that Jesus is alive and actively transforming lives, building the church, and creating disciples. This is what a full, Spirit-filled Christian life looks like.

I had to continually show up at my gym to strengthen my physical muscles. In the same way, as you remain aware and active, you grow stronger spiritually, God ministers in your life daily, and His presence spills out on those around you.

Holy Spirit moves *through* you...

- helping you pray by interceding on your behalf (Romans 8:26-28)

- empowering you to boldly proclaim the Word (Acts 4:8-10; 1 Corinthians 2:4-5; 1 Peter 1:12)

- strengthening you to overcome spiritual opposition (Mark 16:17)

- giving you spiritual gifts to equip you for ministry (1 Corinthians 12:7-11):

words of knowledge	healing	discernment
words of wisdom	great faith	speaking in tongues
prophecy	miracles	interpretation of tongues

Something powerful happens when we experience a genuine move of God. We are different than we were before as Holy Spirit makes us more like Jesus (the Bible word for that is "holiness"). We can't earn more of Holy Spirit by being more religious. We can't muster more of God's power by reading more self-help books. But we can cooperate with Holy Spirit by yielding ourselves to Him.

Sadly, we can also miss out on what Holy Spirit is doing or quench His fiery presence (1 Thessalonians 5:19). Over time, I stopped making time to go to the gym. I got busy, distracted, and disconnected. I stopped placing value on it and missed out on some powerful and transformative growth opportunities.

Act 1 of this book explores some of the ways Holy Spirit communicates. God speaks, and we listen by practicing spiritual disciplines, such as prayer, worship, reading Scripture, Christian meditation, and so on.

If you're waiting to hear the voice of Morgan Freeman booming from the heavens or a choir of angels singing in perfect harmony, you may be waiting a long time. But here's something even better: Every moment is holy as you're empowered by Holy Spirit to view the world through the gospel. Sometimes you hear God within as a still, small voice that's a firm inner prompting with seemingly random thoughts. Other times His voice is roaringly obvious through external situations. My prayer is that this book takes you on an interactive journey that answers the question, What would it look like if we lived fully present to the directions, guidance, and giftings God gives? You'll see fruit produced in your life, and you'll have God-sized adventures and purpose as you participate in His miraculous activity.

SIMPLE PRAYER

Holy Spirit, may we meet You in the pages

of this book. Help us get to know Your

voice, follow Your lead, and grow

in deeper relationship with You.

Amen.

DAY 1 HEARING AID: QUIET TIME

My friend's neighbor had a dog that sounded like a bullhorn. She had to take drastic measures to soundproof her space so she wouldn't lose her sanity. Today's hearing aid is a challenge to soundproof your soul by intentionally quieting the external ruckus. After all, you don't *always* need to listen to music in the car, tune into a podcast during your walk, or reach for your phone for that digital-noise social media scroll.

Sitting in silence isn't scary.

Take some time to consider the natural rhythms of your day and find a few minutes when you can pursue quiet before the Lord. In the shower, as you go for a run, while you make your coffee or do the dishes, in between meetings at work, right before bed…as you pursue quiet, meditate and reflect on His goodness.

JOURNAL PROMPT

Notice it! For the next 24 hours, note each time you reach for a soul-sucking distraction. What were your noisemakers of choice? Also note each time you chose instead to simply be with Holy Spirit in stillness.

How'd it go?

Don't forget to check off this hearing aid on the contents page after you complete it.

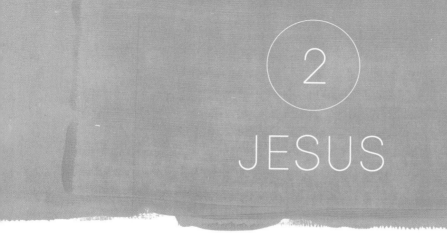

2

JESUS

Faith is the work of God's grace in us. No man can say that
Jesus is the Christ but by the Holy Ghost.

CHARLES H. SPURGEON

"You can't get saved too many times!" my (then) high school friend Brynn joked as she stood up from the altar.

She wiped away the tears after responding to the pastor's message. Brynn had already had a "come-to-Jesus-moment" and been saved…at the ripe old age of four. Now, as a high school student, she felt called to be a missionary, so her response at the altar seemed silly to me. More than 15 years later, I've come to realize that I was the silly one. Salvation happens once, but surrendering to Jesus is a lifestyle, and that's just what Brynn embodied that day.

———————————— ○ ————————————

A prayer repeating the salvation message doesn't save our souls—Jesus does. It's a radical moment that changes everything. My moment happened on a June evening when I was 18. As I watched a church play, Holy Spirit revealed the significance of Jesus to me, and He became the King of my life.

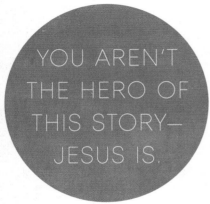

YOU AREN'T THE HERO OF THIS STORY— JESUS IS.

Becoming a Christian isn't something you can earn by praying five Hail Marys before bed or attending church on most Sundays. It isn't something you deserve because you're a middle-class white chick living in the 'burbs of America. You don't deserve to be saved because you get straight As or serve at a soup kitchen. Salvation is a gift; you can't earn it.

Sin takes us out of relationship with God. Jesus's death bridged that gap and gives us new life. He rescued us from our chains of insecurity, pain, and sin. In the most life-changing demonstration of grace, Holy Spirit invites us into relationship with Jesus.

Jesus's life, death, and resurrection have given us hope, purpose, and some awesome promises. When Jesus is your central focus, you begin to hear His voice over your own. You walk with a God-given confidence in the fullness of what He has done for you and what He's continuing to do.

As Brynn demonstrated at the altar that day, following Jesus is a continual process of recognizing and responding to Him daily. When we know Jesus, Holy Spirit empowers us and helps us work out our salvation with fear and trembling (Philippians 2:12 NIV).

The message of the gospel is foundational to hearing God's voice because it reminds you that it's not about *you* anymore. You aren't the hero of this story—Jesus is. The only way you receive that message is by encountering the same Holy Spirit who led, empowered, and anointed Jesus.

You hear God by encountering Jesus. Whether crying at church as we recognize the powerful work of sanctification throughout our lives or praying boldly for the healing of thousands in Africa, let's be accustomed to responding to the move of God. Let's learn to trust and respond to Holy Spirit as He moves and shapes the spaces of our hearts and souls and know that *Jesus* is the one who carries the power to set us free again and again and again.

If you have yet to have a moment of truly surrendering your life to Jesus, I trust Holy Spirit will reveal Himself to you for the first time in a moment of salvation. I also believe He'll continue to reveal Himself to you as you pursue a life of sanctified purpose.

This relationship with Jesus sets us apart and is the design behind our deliverance. It's a lifestyle of freedom that dances in truth to the tune of the gospel. It's walking hand in hand with Jesus, and when a painful circumstance knocks you down, He lifts you up. When you are Spirit-filled, you hear the whispers of comfort and hope over the noise of chaos and despair. You risk loving wholeheartedly and passionately as you proclaim Holy Spirit's promises in broken situations and celebrate Jesus's victory with praise. As we recognize Jesus as the hero of our story, we gear up for the mission and make an impact for Him.

FUN FACT

The apostle Paul knew what it took to transform a culture. He wrote a letter to his companion Titus, encouraging him to empower the people of Crete to change their sinful and harmful ways. We can reflect on this passage in Titus 3 to remind us that when we embrace sound doctrine and are rooted in the truth of the gospel, everything changes through the work of Holy Spirit.

> *Once we, too, were foolish and disobedient. We were misled and became slaves to many lusts and pleasures. Our lives were full of evil and envy, and we hated each other. But—*
>
> *When God our Savior revealed his kindness and love, he saved us, not because of the righteous things we had done, but because of his mercy. He washed away our sins, giving us a new birth and new life through the Holy Spirit. He generously poured out the Spirit upon us through Jesus Christ our Savior. Because of his grace he made us right in his sight and gave us confidence that we will inherit eternal life (Titus 3:3-7 NLT).*

DAY 2 HEARING AID: JESUS

"Jesus told me I shouldn't serve in kids' ministry because it doesn't align with my giftings."

Have you ever pulled the "Jesus card"? That's what we're doing when we act as if Jesus stamped His approval on something. Jesus was fully God and fully man while on earth. We can't follow His example perfectly this side of eternity, but we can look to Him as a model for our lives. So let's play a fun game for today's challenge.

Below is a list of "Jesus told me..." statements. Read each one and determine whether it reflects Jesus's character and aligns with Scripture.

- O Jesus told me to divorce my husband because I fell in love with another dude who has muscles.

- O Jesus told me to make you this green bean casserole because you just had a baby.

- O Jesus told me to leave my job, stop working, and trust Him to provide for my family.

- O Jesus told me to spend my day off helping my grandma go grocery shopping.

Need a hint? Read 2 Thessalonians 3:10.

JOURNAL PROMPT

Now write out your own statement: "Jesus told me…"

Next, ask Holy Spirit…

Does this align with the character of Jesus?

Does this align with Scripture?

Is this God's voice? Does it sound like His will?

When you live a Christlike life, you demonstrate Holy Spirit's power at work in you. (Although, no one loves green bean casserole, so I'm pretty sure that wasn't His idea.)

Don't forget to check off this hearing aid on the contents page after you complete it.

3

THE BIBLE

If you're not being discipled by the Holy Spirit through the written Word of God, you're unknowingly choosing to be discipled by a culture whose humanistic values are subtly pivoting the paradigm of an entire generation. A little leaven leavens the whole, and at the end of the day, one degree of error is still error.

CHRISTOPHER COOK

"If God is everywhere, is He in my poop?"

If you're a parent with young kids, you may write down the funny, smart, and deep things they say when they're little. That previous question came up when we were potty training one of our kids.

Of course, I didn't respond with a simple yes or no. I think I said something about how God doesn't always cause the poopy things to happen in life, but He is certainly with us when they occur.

Some of our kids' comments have been a little off base theologically. "You don't know *everything*, Mom—only Jesus and Santa *Awkward.* know everything."

Most recently my seven-year-old said something that I've been weighing in my mind since. "Sometimes when I read the Bible, the earth seems really small." *Let's start a slow clap for that one.* God's Word puts things into perspective, especially our place in this world.

> *For the word of God is living and active, sharper than any two-edged sword, piercing to the division of soul and of spirit, of joints and of marrow, and discerning the thoughts and intentions of the heart (Hebrews 4:12).*

The whole Bible shows Christ, displays how *big* God really is, and basically slaps us upside the head and reveals whether we're spiritually alive or dead.

in the best way possible

We don't need Oprah's voice playing on loop in our mind or a pep talk from a girl who has to wash her face—the Bible is the clearest way God speaks into our life.

The Word is God-breathed truth that teaches the character of Christ, helps develop a Spirit-led lifestyle, and empowers us to walk in intention. Second Timothy 3:16-17 (NLT) reads, "All Scripture is inspired by God and is useful to teach us what is true and to make us realize what is wrong in our lives. It corrects us when we are wrong and teaches us to do what is right. God uses it to prepare and equip his people to do every good work."

You become what you consume, and whatever you are consuming, consumes you. For example, feast on fast-food tacos for *every* meal, and you'll be a crisp bite away from greasy skin and high cholesterol.

Grab that highlighter!

Watch X-rated stuff, and you'll fixate on those images and on satisfying sexual desires *(don't even get me started)*.

How about this one—we consume so much technology these days. What are you filling your soul with?

- ○ I'm becoming addicted to approval from others through social media likes.
- ○ I'm becoming anchored to Christ by getting in the Word.

When you dig into the Bible, your soul becomes focused on Jesus and fastened to truth. Your heart and mind start to feel the weight of what you're consuming and transform into what is good and holy. Reading the Bible aligns your natural mind with the supernatural.

As you get to know God's voice through Scripture, remember this:

- Test everything against the Word. God's spoken word will *never* contradict His written Word.
- The Bible is true even if it makes you uncomfortable.
- From Genesis to Revelation, Jesus is revealed.
- The Bible shows the big picture of creation, fall, redemption, and restoration.
- Don't cherry-pick verses to complement your desires or goals. Read portions of Scripture in the context of the surrendering verses and chapters as well as the big picture.
- Dive deep! Take time to study phrasing, word usage, and the cultural context. Don't leave the nerdy stuff to your pastor—study the Word for yourself!
- We make time for the things we value. Value how God speaks and honor Him as you prioritize studying the Bible.
- Ask Holy Spirit to make the Word come alive to you as you read. *He likes to answer this prayer!*

Sometimes when I pray through a situation and wait for Holy Spirit's still, small voice, I *feel* as if God is voiceless. Have you ever felt that way? You spill your guts to Father God but feel as if there's no response. Just dead air.

When you can't determine what He is *saying*, dwell on what He has *said.* Our feelings don't dictate whether God is speaking. Reading the Bible is a guaranteed way to get to know God's voice. God is speaking; the question is,

READING THE BIBLE ALIGNS YOUR NATURAL MIND WITH THE SUPERNATURAL.

are we listening? In Scripture, you'll find the words of the Lord you can always count on.

Studying the Word will strengthen your faith in Christ and knowledge of Him while empowering you to answer those hard-hitting theological questions from your kids. Holy Spirit may also use it to highlight certain verses to share with a friend or to shift your prayers, thoughts, and desires in a new direction as you begin to recognize His voice more clearly. Weigh everything you think you hear God say against Scripture. It's too weighty not to.

SIMPLE PRAYER

Lord, may we hear You speak
loud and clear through Your Word.

Amen.

DAY 3 HEARING AID: BIBLE

The search for truth starts with the Word. Today's challenge is to study John 4:1-26 for at least 15 minutes. Sit with the Scripture without looking at a commentary or other materials. Ask Holy Spirit to bring the text alive as you study. *Of course, it isn't really about time.*

JOURNAL PROMPT

As you read, write brief responses to these questions in your journal:

Who are the main characters?

What is the main theme?

What is God revealing about His character?

What does this reveal about Jesus's mission?

What is the meaning of this passage?

Ask Holy Spirit, *How can I apply this to my life?* Write down whatever you feel He's saying.

Don't forget to check off this hearing aid on the contents page after you complete it.

4

THE CHURCH

The church I lead could have the least gifted people,
the least talented people, the fewest leaders, and the least money,
and this church under the power of the Holy Spirit could
still shake the nations for his glory.

DAVID PLATT

As we learn to hear God's voice, we'll also learn to value and love the church, just as He does (Ephesians 5:25).

Church can be a sacred place where people gather to encounter a holy God. There we are challenged and comforted, and we find community and leadership to help us navigate the seasons of life. What does it look like to be a part of a healthy church that functions the way God designed?

The Bible says the function of the church is to "equip the saints for the work of ministry" (Ephesians 4:12). The church isn't just a physical building, but a body of believers. In this chapter, we'll look at what happens when believers come together to worship, learn from God's Word, pray, and participate in helpful ordinances like baptism and communion.

FUN FACT

"Attending church online" isn't attending church.

You're not going to church when you scroll through a few Christian websites. Online sermon-hopping may lead you to some really helpful resources, but that's no substitute for regularly meeting with a group of people and pastoral leaders who point you toward biblical truth. We don't need to get legalistic about church attendance, but let's not get lazy either.

> *Christ himself gave the apostles, the prophets, the evangelists, the pastors and teachers, to equip his people for works of service, so that the body of Christ may be built up until we all reach unity in the faith and in the knowledge of the Son of God and become mature, attaining to the whole measure of the fullness of Christ.*
>
> *Then we will no longer be infants, tossed back and forth by the waves, and blown here and there by every wind of teaching and by the cunning and craftiness of people in their deceitful scheming. Instead, speaking the truth in love, we will grow to become in every respect the mature body of him who is the head, that is, Christ. From him the whole body, joined and held together by every supporting ligament, grows and builds itself up in love, as each part does its work (Ephesians 4:11-16 NIV).*

———————————— ◯ ————————————

A healthy, Christ-centered church functioning with the five roles highlighted above empowers our faith to flourish. Sometimes people exercise these roles and giftings from the pulpit, but more often they operate behind the scenes—at leadership meetings, during Bible studies, and in community service projects, or across the backyard fence, for example. The church is a safe place to get to know God's voice as we learn how to serve everywhere we have been given influence. *Yes, we're called to minister wherever we are.* The church builds up believers so we can represent Jesus to those who don't know Him. This is how Holy Spirit invites us to influence the culture for Him.

If you read through the New Testament book of Acts, you'll see the church grow in numbers as God makes Himself known *We'll dive into* through preaching, hospitality, generosity, miracles, healings, *this later.* and everyday people empowered by Holy Spirit to share the truth of the gospel. God didn't stop giving spiritual gifts at the last book of the Bible. He continues to distribute them today, and ideally, they often operate when the church gathers.

Here are just a few ways I've heard God's voice through leaders and experiences at church. As you continue to read this book, you'll hear more stories. My hope is that you'll have your own too.

God speaks through...

Sermons that teach us how to apply God's Word to shape our lives. I was invited to share the gospel with women who were survivors of sex trafficking. I could not comprehend what they had experienced, and I felt ill-equipped to speak to their hurt. But on a Sunday morning, my pastor taught us verse by verse from Genesis 34. He had been preaching through the Bible and had arrived at a dark passage that deals with sexual assault and rape. This was the *same day* I was going to serve these women. Holy Spirit made the Bible come alive in a new way for me. I entered church feeling ill-equipped and left feeling God-equipped to understand the depths of the Father's love, and I was able to serve out of that love.

Biblical counsel from a pastor or other leader. My husband and I were facing a big decision for our family. We met with a member of our pastoral staff, and through him, God gave us courage and comfort and empowered us to move into new adventures for our family.

Prayer. During a church service, as a leader began praying for me, out came God-breathed words that confirmed a career move I felt God was inviting me to pursue and affirmed the secret, God-given dreams of my heart.

Service. Our church has provided practical support, prayers, and kindness to a friend in our community who faced a tragic accident with their child.

Miracles. A woman after a church service shared that she had a long-term back problem that caused a lot of pain. We prayed a simple prayer, asking God to heal her. God responded miraculously (without any lightning or angel choirs). She returned to her seat free of pain, and we were all awestruck by Him that day!

A CHURCH THAT'S BUILT ON CHRIST IS BUILT UP AS HOLY SPIRIT IS POURED OUT.

Church was never meant to be a place of contention, but of connection to Christ. A church that's built on Christ is built up as Holy Spirit is poured out. Make it a high priority to attend your local church *and serve* with your talents and God-given gifts.

God is speaking and moving in churches around the globe, so let's show up and take part. After all, participating in church is not just about what you can receive but also about what you can give. What if God wants to speak through *you* for someone else's benefit? Are you available, ready, and present to be His mouthpiece?

DAY 4 HEARING AID: CHURCH

Go to church! Today's challenge may extend over to the weekend. Attend your church. If you don't have one, do some research and find a gospel-teaching church in your community.

JOURNAL PROMPT

List some ways you have heard God speak and seen Him move in or through...

- ○ a sermon
- ○ people
- ○ worship
- ○ you

Don't forget to check off this hearing aid on the contents page after you complete it.

5
WORSHIP

To worship God in truth is to recognize Him for being who He is, and
to recognize ourselves for what we are.

BROTHER LAWRENCE

What are you worshipping? Worship gives us a vertical view toward God and a horizontal view of ourselves and others. From our worries to our work, God takes great delight as we lay our concerns aside to give Him center stage and bring Him praise and adoration. We begin to see what or who we revere.

Genuine worship is a lifestyle of glorifying God in the natural realm that reaches into the supernatural. We can worship as we repair the car, play with the kids, or work on a report with our friends. Celebrating and honoring God while performing the task set before us is an act of worship.

Do you remember the story in the Bible of Jesus asking the Samaritan woman for water? You studied it in your day 3 hearing aid. Here's a little more context.

Jesus calls out the woman for having five husbands (John 4:18). Instantly, the woman recognizes Jesus as a prophet, and she asks why Jerusalem is the only place of worship. Jesus explains that she's missing the point:

The time is coming—indeed it's here now—when true worshipers will worship the Father in spirit and in truth. The Father is looking for those who will worship him that way. For God is Spirit, so those who worship him must worship in spirit and in truth (John 4:23-24 NLT).

True worship happens in the visible, physical space as well as the unseen, spiritual realm. God is always active, so supernatural stuff happens all around us all the time. It's just behind the scenes—we typically can't see it, and we usually don't understand it. Worship is one of the ways we bridge that gap.

Whether our worship is expressed through song—hands raised, twirling, and dancing—or deeply reflective, we're laying down our priorities at God's footstool and praising Him as Savior. What would it look like if we worshipped God without an agenda, with great awe for who He is and with little concern for what He can do for us? It shifts our focus to Christ's finished work on the cross. From that place of worship, we hear God speak. As we draw near to Him, He draws near to us, and we catch a glimpse of heaven.[4]

WORSHIP SHIFTS OUR FOCUS TO CHRIST'S FINISHED WORK ON THE CROSS.

In addition to being a lifestyle and a way for us to delight in God, worship is a weapon of warfare. It's a tool we use on the front lines of battle. Our best weapon against the enemy is to turn our attention to the victory Christ already won. As young David worshipped with music, an evil spirit left King Saul.[5] This is an example of the breakthrough that can happen as our worship releases Holy Spirit to produce greater freedom in our lives.

As you're worshipping, do you ever feel a significant change in your thoughts or body? The Lord's solution for a difficult situation may come to you, or your heart may be softened so you can feel God's love and power in a deeper way. It's as if an always active, unseen God becomes seen and felt. The natural collides with the supernatural.

One time during worship at church, a seemingly random prayer and Bible verse came to mind and wouldn't go away. I wrote them down and began to wonder if this was just for me or also for another individual or even the congregation. I slipped over to one of our leaders and asked their opinion… and they handed me a mic!

Of course, I was super nervous, but it was comforting to know the church had a system in place for moments like this. Trying to play it cool, I waited for a nod from the worship leader, and then I shared the Bible verse and began to pray. Soon, Holy Spirit peace flooded the room. Some people responded through tears, and others engaged in quiet reflection. Unknown to me at the time, those words also communicated the main theme of the message that was about to be preached a few minutes later.

Your personal worship and church experience may be different from mine. But as you worship, God can quiet the chaos in your soul, and you just might feel encouraged by a Bible verse like I did. Before you grab a mic and start freestyle rapping verses from the pulpit, consider contacting a church leader during the week and asking what you should do in a similar situation. Is there a system in place? If you feel a God thought or Holy Spirit nudge that might encourage the whole congregation, would the pastor like you to quietly let them know? Would they prefer that you talk with them or another leader after the service?

Your position for battle is on your knees in worship. When you magnify Christ, you make room for God to manifest His presence. If God can use tone-deaf worshipping-Jenny to prayerfully communicate His heart, He can definitely use you too. It starts by living a life of worship.

DAY 5 HEARING AID: WORSHIP

> *Shout joyful praises to God, all the earth! Sing about the glory of his name! Tell the world how glorious he is. Say to God, "How awesome are your deeds! Your enemies cringe before your mighty power. Everything on earth will worship you; they will sing your praises, shouting your name in glorious songs"* (Psalm 66:1-4 NLT).

Ready to sing it loud and proud, my friend? Turn on some worship music and spend time lifting up God's name. Focus fully on worship for three or four songs, and ask Holy Spirit to show you how to hear God's voice as you worship.

JOURNAL PROMPT

What did you notice as you tried to enter into a place of worship?

What was on your mind the whole time?

At the end of your worship experience, were you grateful you spent time in this way?

Don't forget to check off this hearing aid on the contents page after you complete it.

6

CIRCUMSTANCES

You need to return to the truth of God's Word that will last forever,
not meditate on circumstance that will fade and change.

CHRISTINE CAINE

Have you ever misinterpreted God's voice in situations that resulted in heart-break or led you to question God?

o *Yes. Ouch.*   o *Who, me? Never!*

Our theology can easily get confused when we misunderstand what God is saying to us. I know firsthand. Years ago, I tried pulling the Jesus card, interpreting my circumstances as God's stamp of approval on an unhealthy relationship. It didn't work out, and much later, that guy landed in jail.

When we're trying to understand God's plan for our lives, the circumstances right in front of us don't tell the whole story. We must also use the eyes of faith to look beneath the surface of things. God is always moving and orchestrating things behind the scenes. The question is, as we consider how God might be moving in our circumstances, do we do so in a reasonable, mature way? Or instead, do we often misinterpret what's really going on?

Today we're looking at the ways God speaks to us through the circumstances of our lives. This is a tricky topic because decision-making is such a complicated process. We receive input from our feelings, our past experiences, influence from others, what we see unfolding right in front of us, and how we think God is leading.

God's voice can come to us through everyday events that He orchestrates. These "coincidences" may provide comfort and confirm God's plan. Often, He uses seemingly ordinary circumstances, like one door closing as another opens. Sometimes God will use extraordinary circumstances to guide us, such as dreams at night, visions, signs, or a divine harmony of events.

We all suffer from nearsightedness. All we can see are the natural circumstances right in front of us. But the part we can't see—the spiritual realm—is so much bigger. Occasionally, things come into focus, and we catch a glimpse of what God is doing.

One night I had an elaborate dream that gave insight into a real-life situation I was facing. I had made an important decision but felt stuck in a holding pattern, unable to go forward. God used that dream to speak to me about why I had been immobilized and how I could trust Him more. I woke up feeling a deep peace that guided my next steps, and I can only attribute that to God.

Life's circumstances can be confusing—like the time your "soul mate" dumped you or when you had to choose between multiple job offers. If we aren't careful to assess these situations in a mature way, things can get confusing or unhealthy in a hurry. Here are some things to keep in mind as you listen for God's voice in your everyday life.

First things first. Interpret your circumstances in light of the Word of God, His character, the direction you've received through your trusted church leaders, and God's still, small voice.

There may be more than one good option. Like any loving father, God gives His children opportunities to make choices. For example, just as I sometimes let my kids pick which restaurant we go to, God may be inviting you to decide what town to live in. If you're facing a few good options and can't tell which way He's leading, He may be asking you to decide.

Keep a firm grip on God, not on your understanding. What happens when we are absolutely convinced something is a "God thing," but then it ends up not working out? We can be left wondering where God went. Let's make sure we're clinging to God, not to the things we want to happen. ← *That'll preach!*

Don't overspiritualize every circumstance. *Why didn't I get that front-row parking spot?* Does that mean you need to repent from a sin you might have committed eight years ago? More likely, somebody just got there first. Or maybe the other person needed it more than you.

→ **"Throw out a fleece."** This line comes from Judges 6, where Gideon asked

And then consider throwing it to the curb.

for a sign to confirm God's leading. For example, while playing basketball you say, "Okay, God, if I make this next shot, that means You want me to ask Trina on a date." I will admit I've done this (not about Trina, but other things). But I've since decided not to treat God like a genie in a bottle. I pray for wisdom and strengthened faith instead.

Don't stamp every favorable circumstance as God's direction. Your definition of "favorable" may be drastically different from God's.

If you're making a big life change, turn to page 13 and "Check Yourself Before You Wreck Yourself."

We grow in maturity as we learn to identify God's leading and navigate circumstances with discernment. Sometimes a closed door or missed opportunity is divinely orchestrated, just like an open door with your name on it can be. When God closes a door, maybe He's steering you toward a better option that you don't even know about yet.

God causes everything to work together for the good of those who love God and are called according to His purpose (Romans 8:28 NLT).

The extraordinary circumstance I mentioned earlier with the dream at night was a catalyst to move me forward. From there, I talked with a trusted friend about the dream, and I weighed the decision against the Word, which further confirmed how God was speaking and directing my steps. Maybe you too have heard God speak through circumstances and were able to navigate your next steps with maturity and wisdom.

God has given you and me roles to play in God's big story, and that adds a lot of meaning to the circumstances of our lives. But we can't see the whole picture from beginning to end. That's why we need to hold our understanding of our circumstances loosely and hold on to Christ as tight as we can. If you build your theology on your circumstances rather than Christ, you'll have an identity crisis.

IF YOU BUILD YOUR THEOLOGY ON YOUR CIRCUMSTANCES RATHER THAN CHRIST, YOU'LL HAVE AN IDENTITY CRISIS.

Whether things feel out of whack or work out in an amazing way, continue to ask yourself, *What is true about God apart from this circumstance?* That is what sustains us. Our hope doesn't come from an external perspective, but an eternal one.

SIMPLE PRAYER

Holy Spirit, we ask for wisdom, discernment, and peace as You speak to us through the circumstances of our lives. Amen.

DAY 6 HEARING AID: CIRCUMSTANCES

Spend some time asking Holy Spirit to heal your nearsighted vision and help you see how God is speaking through your circumstances.

JOURNAL PROMPT

How has God spoken to you through your everyday circumstances?

Do you struggle to notice God's direction in everyday circumstances?

How has God spoken to you through extraordinary circumstances, such as dreams, visions, or miraculous moments?

Gut check: Do you really think it's possible that God could speak through extraordinary circumstances?

After journaling through these prompts, check off this hearing aid on the contents page.

7

PEOPLE

I sought to hear the voice of God and climbed the topmost steeple,
but God declared: "Go down again—I dwell among the people."

JOHN HENRY NEWMAN

Pastor Mark Shilling and I were discussing the topic of this book when he said, "Fundamentally the world is not opposed to the power of the Holy Spirit. They are opposed to the weirdness of some Christians." ← *Read that again and cue the slow clap.*

As I learn to hear God's voice and grow, I've found myself in some pretty interesting situations. Let me tell you, I've experienced my share of weirdness. Have you too?

○ Yes.　○ No.　○ Maybe. *I'm starting to feel like you're weird right now, Jenny.*

Today we'll consider the possibility that God might speak to you through other people. On day 18 we'll turn it around and talk about the prospect of God speaking through you to others.

I was once invited to teach a Bible study at a church. I don't remember being told in advance that I would be the youngest person in the room—and one of only a few women.

I thought things were going well until suddenly, as I was midsentence, a man I'd never met began cussing me out and yelling that God wanted me to know how horrible I was.

I did the only logical thing to do—I ran away crying. ← *This was not a holy moment. It felt horrible.*

The man followed me outside into an empty field, yelling threats and calling me every demeaning name he could think of. The meeting ended with the man's friend blaming Satan for the outburst and said, "Welcome to ministry."

Dramatic pause.

When God really wants to correct or convict me, He doesn't typically get all up in my face in a chaotic smackdown from a stranger. First Corinthians 14:33 (NIV) assures us that "God is not a God of disorder," and we know that self-control is a fruit of Holy Spirit's presence.

And then there's Old Man McGee. OMG knocked on my door to tell me he had a word from God for my husband and me. He began discussing Revelation, numeric codes, and government conspiracies. Of course, OMG could have had a word from God for us. But after further investigation, we discovered he *Insert shrug emoji here.* → had isolated himself from his entire family and rejected church leaders. *I appreciate your passion, but no thanks.*

FUN FACT

Just because someone said something doesn't mean it's sound. As we trust Holy Spirit to speak through people, we can also trust Him to give us wisdom to accept or reject other people's words as we discern His truth. Test all things! First John 4:1 says,

> Do not believe everyone who claims to speak by the Spirit. You must test them to see if the spirit they have comes from God. For there are many false prophets in the world (NLT).

Sometimes people think God is speaking through them, and it's just weird. Other times, God really *does* speak through people, as weird as it might seem. If you and I were sitting at a campfire, I could share s'more stories of the weird and wonderful ways God has spoken to me through other people. You probably have your stories too. I've learned that there is a relationally appropriate way to honor God and people.

I know God has used people to communicate His comfort or bring confirmation to me. As those people spoke, they reflected God's character and affirmed His Word. For example, God has often used my own family to speak Holy Spirit-fueled words in the simplest and yet most profound ways. One day when I felt defeated after an event for my work, my then four-year-old son, who didn't know how I was feeling, looked at me and said, "I feel like God wants you to know that you did a really good job, Mom."

When I was in the middle of a battle with depression in my college years, a stranger walked up after church and handed me a handwritten note. It was as if she knew my whole situation, even though she didn't know a single thing about me. She spoke life-giving words into depression and pain. I wept as I soaked in the encouragement and truth. In that moment, I felt seen by God through a flesh-and-blood, Spirit-led stranger.

Some of these moments may seem small, others big, but they were all moments that marked my timeline with a nod from God.

> *Most important of all, continue to show deep love for each other, for love covers a multitude of sins. Cheerfully share your home with those who need a meal or a place to stay. God has given each of you a gift from his great variety of spiritual gifts. Use them well to serve one another. Do you have the gift of speaking? Then speak as though God himself were speaking through you. Do you have the gift of helping others? Do it with all the strength and energy that God supplies. Then everything you do will bring glory to God through Jesus Christ. All glory and power to him forever and ever! Amen (1 Peter 4:8-11 NLT).*

GOD USES PEOPLE TO SPEAK AND PROVIDE A HEAVENLY WINK.

As Pastor Mark said, "The world is not opposed to the power of the Holy Spirit." God uses ordinary people in extraordinary ways all the time. Maybe it happens while your accountability partner talks with you about areas you're struggling in, or when a stranger smiles kindly as your kids run around the grocery store like crazy lunatics. These things seem simple but carry a profound impact. You feel seen. God speaks to us through other people's actions: their encouraging insight, their wise counsel, their hospitality, their generosity, or their proclamation of the Word.[6] God uses people to speak and provide a heavenly wink.

SIMPLE PRAYER

Lord, give us ears to hear
You speaking to us through
other people. Amen.

DAY 7 HEARING AID: PEOPLE

Think of a time when God used someone to speak words of life, comfort, conviction, or encouragement to you. Take time to recall as many details of the situation as you can.

JOURNAL PROMPT

How did you know God was speaking through this person?

How did the person's words compare with God's Word and His character?

How did the experience make you feel?

Can't think of anything? Pray and ask Holy Spirit to highlight a time you talked with a mentor, friend, or accountability partner. When you're done, check this off as completed on the contents page.

PRAYER

We serve a God who is waiting to hear from you,
and He can't wait to respond.

PRISCILLA SHIRER

You made it to day 8, and it's time to celebrate! Confetti to your face and high fives coming at you! I'm so proud of you for creating space to hear God's voice last week. You've done a lot of heavy lifting so far while learning to recognize God's voice. You've explored how He speaks through Holy Spirit, Jesus, the Bible, church, worship, our circumstances, and other people. Today, we'll look at one of the foundational disciplines of our faith.

MC Hammer wrote a song about it.

There's a day dedicated to it in the USA.

And you sometimes fall asleep doing it…

Prayer.

———————— ○ ————————

Months ago, with our New York house under contract, Matt and I ventured to the orange-loving state (Florida, in case you didn't catch that) on the hunt for a new place to call home. We had been prayerfully contemplating a move for years, hoping to trade the snow for the sand. We were in pursuit of a sunnier quality of life for our family and relief from the seasonal depression and anxiety my husband was struggling with.

We worked through this decision and pursued God's will as we prayed, talked with our people and church leaders, and experienced many circumstances that gave us peace to move forward. Yet as we were road tripping back from our Florida find-a-home adventure, I wondered, *Is this really the right move for our family, or are we were ruining our kids' lives?* Just like that, my peace was replaced with made-up problems. *I hate oranges, so obviously I won't fit into the culture. What if we become alligator bait or shark meat?*

> PRAYER SHIFTS OUR WILL TO GOD'S WILL AND TURNS OUR GAZE TO HIM.

As fast as the thoughts flooded in, there was a drive-by.

A white semitruck with a cartoon boy painted on the back drove by. The boy was pointing all up in my face with giant words scribbled on the side: "DID YOU PRAY TODAY?"

Let's pause for a hot second and just laugh at this circumstance unfolding. Matt and I finally have forward momentum on a move we've been praying about for years, and here I am creating all the worst-case sceneries. That's so... *human* of me, huh? And then God is just *so* God and reminds me to pray in the middle of my uncertainty.

If we look at the example of Jesus, we see that He frequently retreated from people, daily activities, and other distractions to pray to Father God. He fasted for 40 days and 40 nights in the wilderness.[7] He often retreated to a lake or mountain.[8] His ministry was fueled by these times of intimacy.

To go without something and listen to God.

Here I was, contained in a car for 16 hours, anxiety rising, and the only things I was retreating to were coffee and what-ifs. I was so distracted by my own thoughts and hypothetical pending doom that I forgot to turn my attention to God in prayer. I had to be shaken to attention by the drive-by cartoon-guy to center myself, to take my focus off myself. That's the beauty of prayer. It shifts our will to God's will and turns our gaze to Him.

Pray then like this:

"Our Father in heaven, hallowed ← To be honored as holy.
    be your name.
Your kingdom come,
your will be done,
    on earth as it is in heaven.
Give us this day our daily bread,
and forgive us our debts,
    as we also have forgiven our debtors.
And lead us not into temptation,
    but deliver us from evil" (Matthew 6:9-14).

Studies show that prayer is the most common spiritual discipline in America.[9] I wonder, how much of that time do we spend moaning, "woe is me"? When we run to God, how often do we treat Him like a genie in a bottle, wishing He'd drop us a bazillion dolla dolla bills, y'all? Communication with God is so much more than that. Prayer is meditative, active listening and connecting with God, as Jesus instructed in Matthew 6.

Are you struggling to believe that a personal God is speaking in your everyday life? Try turning down the distractions in your life and practice listening.

Empowered by Holy Spirit, we pray to celebrate, petition, praise, pause, repent, and listen in to a two-way dialogue with Father God. Prayer is a lifestyle of leaning in and listening. Often in times of prayer, I'll be reminded of Scripture or will feel guided to pray specifically for certain things that are weighing on my heart. As drive-by guy reminded me, let me ask you—did you pray today?

SIMPLE PRAYER

Lord, help us pray Your way.

Amen.

DAY 8 HEARING AID: PRAYER

Where is your favorite place to retreat to during prayer?

Find a place where you can focus and actively pray and listen. If you are unsure of how to pray, ask Holy Spirit to intercede for you (Romans 8:26).

JOURNAL PROMPT

What did God say? (It doesn't have to be deep or life-changing; it can be a simple reminder you needed to hear.)

How does this compare with what the Bible teaches you about God's character?

Don't forget to check off this hearing aid on the contents page when you've completed it.

9

CREATION

God dwells in His creation and is everywhere indivisibly present
in all His works. He is transcendent above all His works
even while He is immanent within them.

A.W. TOZER

In the middle of running errands, my little guy stopped and refused to continue cruising the mall. "Mama, I can't keep going. It's just so beautiful!"

Was Max looking at a herd of puppies dressed up in prom dresses and tuxes, frolicking through fields of lollipops and sunflowers? No. (But please, someone make that happen!) My then three-year-old son was looking up at a dying tree. Garbage cans surrounded the tree as if they were offering a border of protective stank. As I kept walking with his sister to the shoe store, Max insisted on standing in wonderment, amazed by the large tree and its brown, crunchy leaves. As he remained frozen in awe, I began noticing the splendor of nature too. In that moment it was as if God was speaking revelation of His nature within nature.

There's so much God-created beauty to be seen. The Bible says,

> Opposition to truth cannot be excused on the basis of ignorance, because from the creation of the world, the invisible qualities ← *Or the holy attributes.* of God's nature have been made visible, such as his eternal power and transcendence. He has made his wonderful attributes easily perceived, for seeing the visible makes us understand the invisible. So then, this leaves everyone without excuse (Romans 1:20 TPT).

Physical nature is *not* God. However, it's a testimony to God's existence. My husband, Matt, is like many others who feel connected to God in nature more than anywhere else. As we've been setting the foundation for how God speaks, we need to mention that time in creation can lead us to interact with the Creator. Through the visible things He's created, we understand Him as Creator. I wrote about the importance of this in my first book, *Courageous Creative*. Connecting with the creative nature of God stirs us to create as we connect with Him.

> TIME IN CREATION LEADS US TO INTERACT WITH THE CREATOR.

The heavens proclaim the glory of God.
　　The skies display his craftsmanship.
Day after day they continue to speak;
　　night after night they make him known.
They speak without a sound or word;
　　their voice is never heard.
Yet their message has gone throughout the earth,
　　and their words to all the world (Psalm 19:1-4 NLT).

When was the last time you heard God speak in nature? I'll let Matt give you a glimpse into what his experience of hearing God in creation is like.

Plodding through the cool sand, a hint of blue shimmer out in the breaking waves catches my eye as dusk turns to dark. The red tide, an explosion of bioluminescent microorganisms, is in full bloom. I run into the shallow water, leaping forward with my surfboard under my chest, and glide out into deeper water. With each paddle stroke, bluish-white trails of light trace past my fingers like wisps of cool fire. As I catch a wave and exit my top turn, illuminated water droplets spray into the air like fireworks. Bobbing up and down out past the waves, waiting for the next set, I marvel at God's creation. The complexity of its form and behavior points to Him. It bubbles up a desire to be close to God and truly know Him. For me, that's the first step in becoming vulnerable and opening my ears to hear His voice. *If this doesn't make you leap into the deep, shark-infested waters, I'm not sure what will!*

Has the hustle of your season caused your focus to be off and distracted you from God's beauty? From the vast ocean to the slowly dying tree at the mall, the wonder of God is all around us. As we appreciate the beauty of God and all He's built in nature, creation serves as a gentle reminder of His majesty. His fingerprints are everywhere. God's infinite power is proven in the details of His creation. When we quiet ourselves before God and notice the things He's created, we create space for Him to speak about how real and powerful He is.

SIMPLE PRAYER

Lord, help us connect to You

through Your craftsmanship.

Amen.

DAY 9 HEARING AID: CREATION

Pick an adventure below:

Lie on the grass and look at the clouds or stargaze at night.

Watch the sunrise or sunset.

Go for a walk in silence.

Go on a prayer walk with your friend (or kids) and pray for your neighborhood.

Draw a picture or take a photo of your favorite go-to nature spot.

Go surfing.

Go sledding or snowboarding.

Take an early morning hike.

If you are bedridden, get creative with this challenge! Watch a documentary that shares stories of the details in nature.

JOURNAL PROMPT

Have you experienced feelings of awe and wonder in your relationship with God? If so, describe a moment when that happened.

What is God speaking to you as you reflect and meditate on Him?

Don't forget to check off this hearing aid on the contents page when you've completed it.

10

HOW IS GOD
SPEAKING LIFE
TO YOU?

Congrats on making it through act 1 and setting a healthy foundation! Go send a text or message to your accountability partner letting them know how far you made it.

o *Did it!*   o *Nah, I'm lazy.*

In the first act of this book, we explored some of the ways God can speak to you. Let's recap a few of the key takeaways:

O   As Christ-followers, we have Holy Spirit, who speaks, guides, and helps us step in sync with His will for our lives.

O   When Jesus is your central focus, you begin to hear His voice in concert with your own.

O   As you quiet yourself before the Lord throughout your day, you'll notice the still, small voice of Holy Spirit speaking within.

O   The Bible is the clearest way God speaks into our lives. Compare everything you hear God saying with Scripture and Christ's character.

- A church built on Christ is built up as Holy Spirit pours out. You'll hear God's voice in this local church environment.

- Worship shifts our focus to Christ's finished work on the cross.

- We grow in maturity as we learn to discern God's leading and navigate circumstances with wisdom and discernment.

- God uses people to speak and provides a heavenly wink through preaching, generosity, wise counsel, encouraging words, and more.

- Prayer shifts our will to God's and turns our gaze to Him.

- Time in creation leads us to interact with the Creator.

SIMPLE PRAYER

Holy Spirit, as we make time for You,

help us practice our listening skills and learn to

hear Your voice in the stillness or the roar.

Amen.

DAY 10 HEARING AID: FREESTYLE

Let's get a little social! Prayerfully ask God to highlight something special for you to share with a person you know. Maybe God will invite you to write a sweet card for your spouse or prompt you to take your sister to coffee. Maybe God will empower you to communicate some encouraging words to a coworker in the middle of a messy situation. Your challenge is to ask God to speak and to respond to His voice. Whether His voice comes as a whisper or a roar, lean in and trust that He is speaking—and then take a risk to follow through.

JOURNAL PROMPT

Who is God bringing to your mind?

What is God prompting you to share with that person?

After you follow through, reflect on the experience. What was the outcome?

Don't forget to check off this hearing aid on the contents page after you've completed it.

GOD'S HOLINESS
IS GREATER THAN
OUR HOLDUPS
AND HANG-UPS.

ACT 2

HOLDUPS AND HANG-UPS

Lord, may Your presence be our fill.

11

INTRODUCTION TO ACT 2

God desires that we become spiritually healthy enough through faith to have a conscience that rightly interprets the work of the Holy Spirit.

BETH MOORE

We've just begun to scratch the surface of getting to know God's voice.

Raise your hand if this has ever happened to you: You sensed God quietly leading you to do something, you carefully considered the possibilities and weighed all your options…and you said no. Maybe Holy Spirit encouraged you to ditch that addiction, but you waved the white flag of defeat. Or He opened a door to some creative innovation, but stepping through it was just too scary. How about that time you were cruising in your car and God put your bestie on your heart so you could pray for them, but you got distracted singing some old-school New Kids on the Block?

Welcome to act 2: Holdups and Hang-Ups. They come from that plot point in humanity's story line when we stopped listening to God's voice—the fall.

Have you been feeling like you fall a lot lately? Don't worry, God's got you. ↑

Our rebellion against God started in the Garden of Eden and extends beyond today. We know the end of the story; Jesus wins this battle. Things will be fully restored, and now we're en route to full wholeness and restoration.

> The LORD God commanded the man, "You are free to eat from any tree in the garden; but you must not eat from the tree of the knowledge of good and evil, for when you eat from it you will certainly die..."
>
> Now the serpent was more crafty than any of the wild animals the LORD God had made. He said to the woman, "Did God really say, 'You must not eat from any tree in the garden'?"
>
> The woman said to the serpent, "We may eat fruit from the trees in the garden, but God did say, 'You must not eat fruit from the tree that is in the middle of the garden, and you must not touch it, or you will die.'"
>
> "You will not certainly die," the serpent said to the woman. "For God knows that when you eat from it your eyes will be opened, and you will be like God, knowing good and evil."
>
> When the woman saw that the fruit of the tree was good for food and pleasing to the eye, and also desirable for gaining wisdom, she took some and ate it. She also gave some to her husband, who was with her, and he ate it. Then the eyes of both of them were opened, and they realized they were naked; so they sewed fig leaves together and made coverings for themselves (Genesis 2:16-17; 3:1-7 NIV).

In these Scriptures, we see various voices influencing Adam and Eve and guiding their actions. I'm left wondering, what voices have we been responding to lately?

○ God and His gospel truth

○ Satan and his crafty lies

○ people who may have an unbiblical worldview

○ your own self-talk

The serpent, also known as the devil or Satan in Revelation 20:2, twisted God's words. Instead of listening to God, Eve listened to the serpent, and Adam followed along. Then they took action, trying to become more godlike.

What's the big deal? They ate some fruit. Doesn't an apple a day keep the doctor away? The problem wasn't that Adam and Eve ate some fruit but that they responded to the wrong voice, and that separated them from God.

Genesis goes on to reveal that after Adam and Eve ate the fruit, they heard God walking in the garden, and they hid. They once viewed their naked bodies as pure, but now they were ashamed. Feeling the weight of guilt, they isolated themselves from the presence of God. ← *A pretty good description of hell, by the way.*

We're still reeling from that tragedy. Murders, mass shootings, addiction, divorce, disease, death, struggle, sin... Maybe you've been praying for years for a baby, and you feel forgotten by God. Maybe your wife cheated on you, and you're drowning in depression. Or maybe you long for companionship, but you've connected to all the wrong things.

After Adam and Eve disobeyed the voice of God, they played the victim, shifting the blame for their actions. But you and I don't have time to mess around. We're not victims; we're victorious because of Christ. That's why in act 2 we're going to discuss some hard stuff, from sin to suffering, and we'll ask God what He thinks about it. Battle armor on, warrior.

> *We can demolish every deceptive fantasy that opposes God and break through every arrogant attitude that is raised up in defiance of the true knowledge of God. We capture, like prisoners of war, every thought and insist that it bow in obedience to the Anointed One (2 Corinthians 10:5 TPT).*

Let's name the things that have a long-standing history of separating humanity from the presence of God—and punch those things in the face. Some battles, like cancer or loss, come seemingly out of nowhere. We bring other battles on ourselves by aligning with the dominion of darkness instead of the kingdom of heaven. ← *Ouch!*

What happened in the Garden of Eden contaminated humanity. But even when we hide from God, He finds us. Adam and Eve hid in their shame-filled nakedness, but God remained good. He walked them through the consequences of their choices, and then He clothed them (Genesis 3:21).

GOD'S HOLINESS IS GREATER THAN OUR HOLDUPS AND HANG-UPS.

God physically covered them, and the blood of Jesus spiritually covers us. It heals our eternal separation from God and produces life. Remember, we serve a God of redemption and restoration. You can stop hiding now. You already have the solution—it's Jesus.

As we dive into these next couple of days, let's change our mind-set and let God transform our hearts and wills. Let's brave the discomfort of sorting out God's truth from lies and watch as Holy Spirit fills us to overflowing. Let's live out that truth as God walks us into wholeness. Let's view the world through a gospel-centered lens so we can enjoy Spirit-led lives. God's holiness is greater than our holdups and hang-ups, so let's come out of hiding. He's calling our names; let's show up.

SIMPLE PRAYER

Lord, help us stay focused
on You and Your goodness.
Amen.

DAY 11 HEARING AID: QUIET TIME

Spend some quiet time with Holy Spirit to reflect on a few hard things. Take a deep breath, free yourself from all distractions, and take a few minutes to listen to His still, small voice.

JOURNAL PROMPT

Think of a time when you felt the weight of guilt, shame, or sin...

Did you hide from God?

What was the result?

Can you see any ways God showed you His goodness?

If you feel isolated because of guilt, sin, or shame, you can move toward greater intimacy with God today. Those aren't reasons to hide from a loving Father, but reasons to run to Him. Prayerfully reflect on who God is and the forgiveness He gives. He's covering you and is with you.

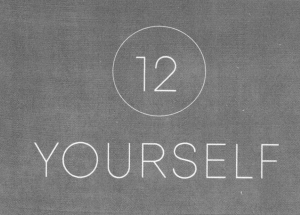

12
YOURSELF

I hope all is well with you and that you are as healthy
in body as you are strong in spirit.

3 JOHN 2 NLT

You and me, we're complex human beings. We are spirits who have souls and live in bodies. We're made up of emotions, needs, wants, beliefs, past experiences, character traits we're born with, talents we develop over time…the list goes on and on. Our view of ourselves can be marvelous and messy.

Like I said, complex!

When you became a Christian, Holy Spirit joined Himself to your spirit (1 Corinthians 6:17) and started transforming your soul (which contains your will, emotions, and mind), thereby guiding your body. Body, soul, and spirit are interconnected. This is why our spiritual health, emotional health, and physical health affect one another so much.

One second we think we're fabulous; the next, we feel like absolute failures. Bouncing between these extremes is a pretty good sign that we're listening to our own voice rather than God's. To bolster our fragile identity, we resort to pep talks or act out of selfishness instead of humble service. We're balancing on a pedestal that wasn't meant to support us.

FUN FACT

Saul, a Pharisee (a.k.a. the apostle Paul), experienced a radical conversion—from murdering Christians to ministering for Christ.

In the book of Acts, we see the apostle Paul transformed into a humble man whom God used to spread the gospel. Paul had supernatural dreams and visions, and he walked in obedience as God directed his steps. Throughout his ministry, he focused on Christ, and signs and wonders followed. Eternal truths shaped his attitude toward his "light and momentary troubles" (2 Corinthians 4:17) and his struggle with sin (Romans 7:21–8:2).

Check out the crazy list in 2 Corinthians 11:23-29!

Like Paul, we have to humble ourselves to have an accurate and healthy view of ourselves. We don't want to be overconfident, but we need to remember we are infinitely valuable. Here are two ways a healthy view of yourself can help you hear God's voice.

First, remember that your struggles don't determine who you are.

Circumstances, anxieties, addictions…these things do not define you. Take the magnifying glass off the unhelpful labels, and magnify Christ instead. Unhealthy labels don't lead to healing—they often hinder it.

IT'S TIME TO GET OVER YOUR SELFIE.

I used to label myself as worthless. For ten years, I heard God inviting me to pursue a specific job, but I resisted. *Who do I think I am to do that?* I felt undervalued, so I underestimated what God could do in and through me. My soul shouted lies that paralyzed me from moving forward.

As I worked through my pain and my mental health began to improve, God continued speaking. When I asked myself, *Who do I think I am?* Holy Spirit interrupted with another question: "Who do you think I AM?"

Second, even though you undoubtedly have an awesome personality, remember that God is the star of the story.

Personality tests are all the rage these days. People introduce themselves with Enneagram numbers and break up over supposedly incompatible personality types. For the love of all things holy, you are more than those personality profiles. Let's become less obsessed with personality tests and more obsessed with who God says we are. Our confidence isn't in ourselves—it's in Christ.

Self-confidence is good. God-confidence is even better. Let's call it "Godfidence!"

FUN FACT

The word "confidence" comes from the Latin words con (with) and fide (faith). Put them together and "confidence" means "with faith." That means Godfidence is "God-faith"—faith in who He is and what He says!

This book is not about how great and mighty you are. It's about how great and mighty God is. We live healthier lives when we understand that because of our relationship with Jesus, our spirit is guided by Holy Spirit, who is in fellowship with the Father. God has a purpose and a plan for you, and that can ignite a passion in you that will influence your world. Let's prayerfully ask God how we can be part of His story rather than begging Him to transform ours. Christ is the solution to our selfishness.

When we put God first, we develop healthy characteristics and experience positive consequences. As we pursue God, we begin to change. The

Actually, as we realize He's pursuing us! ⟶ apostle Paul lived with a servant's heart and followed God's voice, and God transformed and empowered him. The same can happen

to us as we honor God's presence in our lives. It's time to get over your selfie. From a place of humble confidence, we hear direction and counsel. We will experience the miraculous when we pursue Christ simply because of who He is and not what He's creating us to be.

SIMPLE PRAYER

Lord, just like John 3:30 says…

less of me and more of You.

Amen.

DAY 12 HEARING AID: JESUS

In this hearing aid challenge, let's practice listening to Christ over the ruckus of our self-talk. Consider some things you might say to yourself, and then rephrase those thoughts to put the emphasis on Christ. Here are a few examples:

I'm stressed.
"I'm feeling stressed, but I can give my anxiety to Jesus and have confidence in Him because He cares for me."

I'm kind.
"Holy Spirit is developing kindness in my life."

JOURNAL PROMPT

Your turn. What are some phrases you have been telling yourself lately? How can you restate them to keep your focus on Christ?

Remember to check off this hearing aid on the contents page after you complete it.

13

SIN

I once heard the story of a man who was teaching a discipleship class about sin. He was explaining that we all need to address our sin and not brush it under the rug. Wanting to really hit home his main point, he told the class, "In a few seconds, I'm going to commit the worst sin you can imagine."

Naturally, the room held an uncomfortable silence, and the students in the front row began to inch their seats backward.

"Three...two...one..."

The man stood motionless. Not a flinch.

His point? Our biggest sin issue is unresponsiveness. When we think of sins, we think of bigger-than-life actions, like murder or rape or infidelity. But in fact, to sin is to be unfaithful to God, to ignore the voice of Holy Spirit, to not repent...even in the small stuff.

We live sandwiched between the image of God and the brokenness of the fall. The old self and the new are at war. Being a Christian carries the tension of being a saint who constantly sins. In Romans 7, Paul grieves the fact that he often does what he doesn't want to, but he didn't let that define him: "So now it is no longer I who do it, but sin that dwells within me" (7:17).

As Paul said, our identity is not determined by the old sin nature but by the new creations we've become in Christ. This doesn't give us permission to go on sinning, as if we can just throw down the grace card and ignore our mistakes. Instead, we repent, apologizing to God because these sins are *not* who we are anymore. They are in conflict with who God designed us to be. So the question is, is it really a *sin* issue or a *Spirit* issue?

It's both. We face a challenge as we walk with Holy Spirit. It might look like this:

Tina and her husband get in a dumb fight over who's going to do the dishes. She's left feeling hurt, bitter, and undervalued. Later that night she's scrolling through photos on social media and comes across a photo of nice-guy Jimmy, whom she met at church. Yes, church (cue the creepy music).

Tina remembers Jimmy is a coffee snob. She posts a picture of the after-dinner coffee she brewed with locally roasted beans, hoping Jimmy will see it. Her seemingly insignificant cry for attention begins to carry heavy significance. Tina resents her husband and connects with Jimmy in their casual convos. Weeks go by, and Jimmy knows the best coffee place in town, so he invites her to try it. For months, Jimmy gives Tina the attention she wants, leading to an affair that ruins her marriage, hurts everyone in her family, and leaves her feeling isolated from God and other people.

Everyone says, "Oh, I didn't see that coming! I'm shocked—it's so out of character!" Which it is, because she's made in the image of Christ. But do you see how you can trace it back to that first moment? Circle all the moments in the story when Tina could have paid attention to God's voice and followed the Spirit's leading. When was the first time?

When Tina was hurt, she didn't seek Holy Spirit's peace, so the sin of bitterness took root in her soul. She didn't seek the guidance of Holy Spirit when feeling resentment toward her husband. Over time, the crumbs she brushed under the rug attracted an infestation of creepy crawlies. Sin that goes unchecked can manifest all kinds of crazy.

What are the crumbs you're tempted to hide? Acting in greed, speaking ill of the church, laziness, dishonoring your parents, hate, unforgiveness, sexual immorality, cheating, dishonesty, lying, gossip, slander, hypocrisy, bragging, exaggerating the truth, wanting what others have, jealousy, drunkenness, envy... But rather than fixating on those things, let's fixate on the fact that we are children of God, new creations, a temple of Holy Spirit, fearfully and wonderfully made, and forgiven!

> *You, however, are not in the flesh but in the Spirit, if in fact the Spirit of God dwells in you. Anyone who does not have the Spirit of Christ does not belong to him. But if Christ is in you, although the body is dead because of sin, the Spirit is life because of righteousness. If the Spirit of him who raised Jesus from the dead dwells in you, he who raised Christ Jesus from the dead will also give life to your mortal bodies through his Spirit who dwells in you (Romans 8:9-11).*

FUN FACT

The key term in Romans 8 is "Spirit," which Paul uses 21 times throughout Romans 8. Sin does not take away our identity as saints. Nor does being saints make us immune from the consequences of our mistakes. Holy Spirit enables us to deafen sin and hear Him directing us toward victory.

What would it look like if we accepted what Holy Spirit provides and quit reaching for unhealthy substitutes? We don't gain significance by tearing down our sister-friend. We aren't made whole by looking at pornography. We don't find joy, peace, or purpose in coffee with Jimmy that spins out of control and ruins everything. The beauty of the Spirit dwelling in you is that sin does not get to control you.

Let's break up with the lie that we can't talk about sin. We can, so let's do. Let's break up with the lie that our out-of-character behavior brings us good. It doesn't because it isn't.

Let's align with God's Word and the words of conviction that call us to change. We sin. God is Savior over that. He's better than the shame that holds us captive. He's better than the addictions that ravish us. He's better than the superiority we feel when we tear others down.

We are better than that because He designed us to be better. He saved us and calls us saints. Let's respond in repentance, declaring that we love God more than [fill in the blank]. Let's stop letting shame isolate us, and let's hear His voice as He restores our hearts and minds.

SIMPLE PRAYER

Lord, we repent. We love You more than our shame, addictions, and sins that may be causing us to turn from You. Help us develop habits that turn us to Holy Spirit for the peace and purpose we so desperately crave.

Amen.

DAY 13 HEARING AID: BIBLE

Slowly read Luke 7:36-50—a beautiful story of Jesus forgiving sin.

JOURNAL PROMPT

Who are the main characters?

What is the main theme?

What is God revealing about His character?

How do you see the bigger picture of Jesus in this?

What is the meaning of this passage?

Ask Holy Spirit, *How can I apply this to my life?* Write down whatever comes to mind. And don't forget to check off this hearing aid on the contents page after you complete it.

DISTRACTIONS

It takes deliberate and continuous effort to carve out time in our overfull schedules to listen to the voice of God.

SHEILA WALSH

Distractions pull our attention off the things that truly matter. Maybe you are making dinner with your daughter, but you don't interact with her because your mind is hijacked by your to-do list. Or you are sitting in church, but you can't focus on the sermon because you're trying to remember whether you have all the ingredients for the tacos you'll be making when you get home. Don't even get me started on how technology pulls our attention with emails, texts, and social media pop-ups.

I'm not suggesting we ban technology or go all monk and live in solitude. We will always have interruptions and will often need to multitask. But let's learn how to be fully present for at least a few important moments. When we're only halfway there, we overlook things, misunderstand situations, or devalue people.

You feeling me? Sit in silence for a solid 30 seconds.

Did you do it?

    o *No, I almost died.*   o *Yes, and I survived!*

Were you comfortable just *being*? Or was it difficult to stop the mental gymnastics of organizing your to-do list for today?

We live in a cluttered, distracted society, and we develop unhealthy habits of mindlessly reaching for things we should keep out of reach. Think about that for a minute—do you tend to be reckless and rushed in your relationships, or do you take time to be deliberate and reflective? How does our lack of focus affect our intimacy with others? Our intimacy with God?

This became clear to me the night I went for a worship walk.

I love listening to worship music and praying while I walk around town. It's one of my favorite ways to unwind and connect with God. On my walk the other night, I came to a crosswalk, and the pedestrian signal said to stop. There were no cars in sight, and I could have easily Froggered my way across the street and been fine. I felt awkward because there was no reason to stand still except for the red-handed light.

I started to grab my phone to fill the empty mind space, and the Lord totally called me out on it:

"Be comfortable in the waiting."

I began to think of instances in the past few months when I had reached for distractions rather than resting in the moment God was giving me.

Luke 10:40 shares the story of Martha and Mary. Martha was literally serving Jesus, yet "she was distracted by her many tasks." We can be serving and showing up for Jesus all day long but still be distracted from Him.

It happens all the time. In fact, this is one of the biggest battles with hearing God. Maybe we think He wants us to fill every pause with important thoughts or even noble actions. He doesn't.

Think of it like this. When I go on a date with my husband, we want to enjoy some quality time. But if I'm texting or watching sports on a TV on the restaurant wall, I'm preoccupied. I'm being distracted from him even though I'm showing up for him.

Let's take it a step further. My husband and I have a committed relationship. Whether we are in the same room or in different locations, we make decisions that honor our committed relationship. In the same way, believers have a new covenant relationship with Jesus. God dwells among us and in us by His Spirit through His Son, Jesus Christ. Even when we're busy doing everyday stuff and we aren't feeling His presence, we can remain focused and make decisions that honor and place value on the relationship.

Then when we have more focused experiences with God through prayer, worship, reflection, and so on, we can stay attuned and attentive to honor and respond to His voice.

"Be comfortable in the waiting." We may have to replace some bad habits with better practices, but just as you can learn to make space to honor those you love, you can do the same for the One who loves you with an everlasting love.

SIMPLE PRAYER

Lord, help us ditch the

distractions and disturbances

and focus our attention on You.

Amen.

DAY 14 HEARING AID: WORSHIP

Find 20 minutes today to give your full attention to worshipping the Lord. Of course, it isn't about the amount of time—that's just a jumping-off point to get started. Here a few practical ideas to help you prepare:

- O Do a brain dump and make a list of things floating in your mind that could distract you.
- O Silence your phone. Put it in another room.
- O If you have kids who need your attention during this time, invite them to participate.
- O Grab your Bible in case you want to look up a passage.

The goal of this hearing aid is to bring freedom as you make space to focus on Christ. Queue up your favorite worship music or sing spontaneously. Find freedom in your personal worship time today.

JOURNAL PROMPT

How did it go? Was it difficult to focus on Jesus for 20 minutes?

Did anything in particular help you maintain your focus?

15

CONFUSION

There is no neutral ground in the universe. Every square inch, every split second is claimed by God and counterclaimed by Satan.

C.S. LEWIS

We're two weeks into our 31-day interactive journey. I pray that your eyes and ears have been opening and that you have started seeing and hearing God in new ways.

We're still deep in the holdups and hang-ups section of the book. In this chapter, let's call out two misunderstandings that can drown out God's voice and hurt our souls. Confusion surrounds these two issues. Fortunately, the first is easy to answer; the second is a little trickier.

The first misunderstanding is that our failures disqualify us from showing up with God.

Of course, this is a ridiculous lie. We know that a relationship with God has nothing to do with *our* worthiness but everything to do with the One who is worthy. We're the first ones to admit we could never earn the mind-boggling love He constantly pours out on us. No one deserves an invitation to God's presence…but He invites us anyway.

We know all that. But even though we know the truth, we get tripped up because we tend to focus on the first part of the lie—the part about *our failures*.

Like all good lies, this one contains an element of truth: Yes, we mess up and sin. And as if our honest-to-goodness mistakes aren't enough to make us feel unworthy, we also have to deal with the tailor-made lies floating around in our heads that accuse us of being worthless, dumb, horrible parents, or anything else that would make us feel like God would never bother talking to us.

Simply naming these personal lies can help us refute them. Let's bring them out of the darkness and shine some light:

- O Pause right here and make a list of lies that have challenged your God-given identity.

- O Next, prayerfully ask for God's truth-filled response to each lie. *It's important.*

The second misunderstanding is that God has stopped talking.

This second area of confusion is less personal and more theological—and just as harmful. We wonder, *Can I really hear God's voice?* With the Bible in our hands and Jesus's real-life example before us, don't we already have the complete revelation of God? What's to say we're not just making up all these other thoughts?

One reason this is confusing for a lot of people is that good-hearted believers have various opinions about this. Some Christians believe that God's direct, unfiltered interactions with people ended with the Bible. They hold the belief that spiritual gifts disappeared after the time of Jesus's disciples in first-century Christianity.

Why is this view, called cessationism, popular in many churches? These brothers and sisters in Christ focus on the authority and inspiration of Scripture and look only there for wisdom to answer our modern-day questions. In this view, if God were to speak directly to people through the gifts of the Spirit listed in 1 Corinthians 12:7-11, He would be adding to the Word of God. (We'll talk more about spiritual gifts on day 20.)

Other Christians treasure the Bible too, but they also believe that God continues to speak to us today in many ways—through spiritual gifts, in our prayer times, through a sermon at church, through prophetic words, in divinely orchestrated events, and so on. These believers, sometimes referred to as continuists, understand the gifts were not only essential in establishing the church but are also needed for its continual strengthening and maturating today.

Continuists are also hesitant to say what God can't do, *He is God, after all.* and they call attention to the many powerful ways God is moving in the world. Sometimes people pay more attention to the gifts than they do to Scripture, and that can lead to problems. We must remember that our experience in hearing God's voice must never contradict Scripture and that experience doesn't carry more weight than the biblical text.

Here's a passage people usually refer to in this discussion. Take some time to underline all the temporary gifts listed in these verses, and circle all the eternal gifts.

> *Love never fails. But where there are prophecies, they will cease; where there are tongues, they will be stilled; where there is knowledge, it will pass away. For we know in part and we prophesy in part, but when completeness comes, what is in part disappears. When I was a child, I talked like a child, I thought like a child, I reasoned like a child. When I became a man, I put the ways of childhood behind me. For now we see only a reflection as in a mirror; then we shall see face to face. Now I know in part; then I shall know fully, even as I am fully known.*
>
> *And now these three remain: faith, hope and love. But the greatest of these is love (1 Corinthians 13:8-13 NIV).*

Some people believe this passage is saying spiritual gifts aren't for today. But I believe it confirms they are. Here's why. Faith, hope, and love are eternal—they will continue beyond your physical life. Obviously, Holy Spirit is eternal too, but His "power" gifts (prophecy, tongues, and so on) are temporal.

The purpose of the power gifts is to let Holy Spirit minister through you to point people to Christ. So in eternity, if we are already fully restored and face-to-face with Jesus, why would we need those gifts? We won't need healing because we will be fully healed. We won't need a prophetic word about hope because we will be standing in the presence of Hope Himself. We won't need to discern the presence of demons because they will be banished to hell (just sayin'). Those gifts are temporal—they are for us today, right here and right now.

Until Jesus returns, we can't comprehend the fullness of what is to come, but while we wait, He empowers us through Holy Spirit to demonstrate His authority and power on earth. Holy Spirit ministers in and through our lives to heal a broken world.

What if God is just as excited about talking with you as you are with Him? What if those little thoughts that come to you at just the right time are whispers from God's still, small voice? What if that sentence someone said to you in passing *really was* the word of the Lord for you in that moment? What if God is communicating with people today just as He has throughout history?

And what would it hurt to live with that kind of hope?

God gives us spiritual gifts to demonstrate His Word is true. The gifts don't diminish or dismiss the authority, sufficiency, or infallibility of Scripture. They confirm it. That's why we must earnestly desire the gifts (1 Corinthians 12:31) and test all things against Scripture (1 Thessalonians 5:21).

FUN FACT

The book of Acts records about 20 individual miracles and 10 groups of miracles that occurred during a span of about 30 years.

The same Holy Spirit who used Peter to speak words of promise and hope to entire communities can also use a Jesus-loving believer to speak prophetic encouragement, comfort, or edification to a friend. The same God who gives you breath can use your prayer to demolish your mama's diagnosis of lung cancer. The same God who poured out Holy Spirit to bring unity and build up the church can do the very same thing today through His people. ⟵

Let God be fully God over your whole life, not just some parts *And He is!* of it. The enemy's goal is to slyly lead you away from the transformational power of the gospel. Remember, we get to do better in applying the biblical text to our lives daily. Let's live in expectation that Holy Spirit is still using the temporal gifts to work through us to change our world and to demonstrate the Bible as true.

SIMPLE PRAYER

Holy Spirit, we repent for not pursuing You wholeheartedly every day. Sometimes we haven't been open to using the gifts You've given us. Save us from confusion, and help us earnestly desire and pursue spiritual gifts so we can partner with You to change the world around us. Thank You for the amazing things You've done in the past and the even more amazing things yet to come! Amen.

DAY 15 HEARING AID: BIBLE

Read 1 Corinthians 12–14 slowly and thoughtfully.

JOURNAL PROMPT

Who are the main characters?

What is the main theme?

What is God revealing about His character?

How do you see the bigger picture of Jesus in this?

What is the meaning of this passage?

Ask Holy Spirit, *How can I apply this to my life?* Write down whatever comes to mind. And don't forget to check off this hearing aid on the contents page after you complete it.

16

ISOLATION

The Holy Spirit showed me that when I put up walls to keep others out, I also wall myself into a solitary place of confinement.

JOYCE MEYER

How many times do we pull away from people because we're afraid of being too much or not enough, or are too tired to even show up? We're wired for community and need those iron-sharpens-iron relationships. When we isolate ourselves or pull out of friendships and local church communities, we separate from so much that God has for us, and that becomes a hang-up in hearing God's voice. ⟵ *Don't go rogue.*

> *Every believer was faithfully devoted to following the teachings of the apostles. Their hearts were mutually linked to one another, sharing communion and coming together regularly for prayer. A deep sense of holy awe swept over everyone, and the apostles performed many miraculous signs and wonders. All the believers were in fellowship as one body, and they shared with one another whatever they had (Acts 2:42-44 TPT).*

Healthy community encourages spiritual growth. Intentional isolation leads to destruction. Isolation has even been shown to deteriorate our physical well-being. A Harvard article reports,

> *When separated from others, humans find themselves in a psychological stress state some might refer to as "fight or flight." Being around other people provides safety and security that stifles this stress state and decreases the perception of loneliness. When alone, or feeling alone, humans subconsciously sense that they must be more aware of threats in the environment, so the body prepares to deal with them via a stress response.*[11]

One challenge to hearing God's voice in the local church is showing up to listen. "Here's the church, here's the steeple, open the doors..." Let's figure out where all the people are, shall we?

I isolated myself from church because of bitterness. In my early twenties, I was wounded by abusive church leaders. I secluded myself and was reluctant to trust a local church again. But church leaders experience brokenness just like everybody else, and sometimes their own pain affects the way they guide the church. I wonder if you too have been hurt by leaders who are themselves hurting.

Let's not brush poor leadership under the rug. Abuse is wrong. Our pain is real. But the good news is, that doesn't have to be the end of the story. We can be honest about human brokenness and still choose to honor God as He builds the church. Let's talk about the hard stuff and show up for one another, and let's also focus on the beauty of Christ—even His beauty manifested in the (always imperfect) church.

God taught me how to love the local church again, and from that place of healing, I've been active in local churches for 16 years (and counting).

Of course, committing to a local church is different from simply visiting one church after another. Sustained church shopping creates a false sense of fellowship. Consumer Christianity starves the soul and eventually kills converts.

> ISOLATION CREATES SEPARATION, BUT GOD IS INVITING US INTO PARTICIPATION.

Contrast that with the early church in the book of Acts. On the day of Pentecost, Holy Spirit filled an entire community. As they gathered, worshipped, shared meals, and strengthened their faith, the Lord added to their numbers, people were cared for, and they lived generously for Jesus. You aren't created to be alone, so consider taking a step deeper into your church family.

God has given me some wonderful, lifelong relationships that developed in the church community. God has used some of these relationships to speak confirming words and encouragement into my family's life. I've seen Holy Spirit move in radical and powerful ways as people and communities have been restored and reconciled in the love of Christ. If you've been struggling in isolation because of bitterness or hurt, please read a special note just for you from my pastor, Michael Servello Jr.

I am humbled that Jenny would give me the opportunity to address you. In today's reading, she offers hope to those who have pulled back from a local family of believers because of their wounds. Jenny has been open about her own painful experience, but the pain she's experienced hasn't held her back. I can't imagine a family like Jenny's not being part of our local church. What she has added has been nothing short of amazing. In fact, as

I write this, she and her family are preparing to relocate to another state, and we grieve our loss because of their friendship and the gifts they bring.

As a pastor's kid and now a pastor, let me just say, I'm not ignorant of the dark side of church families. Church can be an ugly place. We are all sinners who are becoming more like Christ every day, and that includes pastors. I humbly apologize to you, dear reader, for the hurt that you may have experienced by a church family. Your wound may be deep, but I want to encourage you to humbly forgive and to find healing in a healthy local church—a church that has a plurality of leadership, clear accountability, healthy doctrine, and strong relationships.

Let's remember the heart of Christianity and the foundation of Christian community is the work of Christ and His forgiveness toward us. Because we are imitators of Christ, forgiveness should mark our lives too. Reconciliation with those who have hurt you might not be in the near future, but forgiveness is a must. Pursue a healthy body of believers where you and your family can grow in Christ and experience the joys and pains of covenant relationship.

With prayer and love,
Pastor Mike Servello Jr.

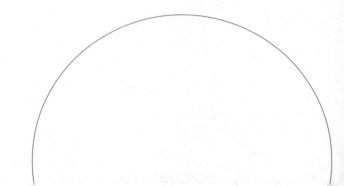

DAY 16 HEARING AID: CHURCH

Today's challenge will likely extend into the weekend. Go to church. When you are there, find someone and schedule a coffee hang or dinner date, or invite them over for a family game night or pizza party. Look through your schedules together and enter the date in your calendars before you leave.

JOURNAL PROMPT

After you hang out with that person, reflect on your time together and write down what comes to mind: How did the Lord encourage you, challenge you, or [fill in the blank] through your time of fellowship?

After you complete this challenge, be sure to check it off on the contents page.

17

CHAOS AND FEAR

Half our fears arise from neglect of the Bible.

CHARLES H. SPURGEON

Have you ever experienced post-traumatic petting zoo disorder?

I was three years old. My dad paid a quarter for an ice-cream cone of feed pellets for the chickens, bunnies, goats, and deer. Then he ushered us into a pit of *hell*.

As I death-gripped that food, I was convinced something else was about to death-grip my face. The deer and goats ran over, circling around me like ravenous lunatics. It was mass chaos, and I was going to be their main course. I yelled just like Kevin McCallister did after he put aftershave on his face in *Home Alone*. There was no fight or flight going on here; I was frozen in fear.

—————— ○ ——————

We experience fear for a reason: When it is based on reality, it helps us survive. But fear can also be irrational, like when our safe, loving, heavenly Father speaks to us…and we feel afraid.

One time I felt impressed that the Lord gave me an encouraging word for a person at church. My first response was that the person would think I was crazy and never talk to me again. (I may or may not have felt this way on more than one occasion.) So I attributed my impression to the spicy tacos I had just eaten, ignored God's voice, and didn't say a word. I later found out that God *was* in fact speaking and that I missed out on a powerful opportunity to demonstrate His love.

Another time, Holy Spirit invited me to a dying man's bedside to pray for him. I went to the hospital and found his room. I peeked in and saw a frail man surrounded by machines...and I left. ← *God can redeem experiences like this when we repent!*

Have you ever heard God's voice and felt afraid? How might you honor your feelings even as you respond in faith?

> *All who are led by the Spirit of God are sons of God. For you did not receive the spirit of slavery to fall back into fear, but you have received the Spirit of adoption as sons, by whom we cry, "Abba! Father!" The Spirit himself bears witness with our spirit that we are children of God, and if children, then heirs—heirs of God and fellow heirs with Christ, provided we suffer with him in order that we may also be glorified with him (Romans 8:14-17).*

When we are controlled by our fear, it's hard to see how God is moving and hear what He is saying. We're afraid to mess it up, get it wrong, say the wrong thing, and step into uncharted waters. But because of our relationship with Jesus, we don't have to be controlled by fear. Fear may be present, but it doesn't have to have the last word. If your fear is taking over your thoughts, remember that fear is not always rational. Look to your loving Father—He will show you the truth and comfort you with His peace.

———————————— ○ ————————————

So what happened in that petting zoo? My dad saw that I was terrified, and with a one-armed swoop, he lifted me off the ground and tucked me into his six-foot-three frame. A photo that was snapped at that moment shows my utter terror and my dad's complete control. One particularly friendly goat is standing on its hind legs, pressing its front legs on my dad's abdomen. My dad was like a goat whisperer.

PERFECT PEACE ISN'T BASED ON OUR PLACE IN THIS WORLD, BUT ON OUR PLACE IN GOD'S ARMS.

This picture illustrates the way we can bring our fears to our heavenly Father. *His love protects us, comforts us, and provides peace.* When we are afraid, we can cry out like children to Abba Father and learn to trust Him as He holds us close. We don't have to remain paralyzed in fear, but can run to God's strong embrace.

We maintain perfect peace by focusing on Him rather than our circumstances, the possible consequences, or our fear itself. Peace is who He is. *Perfect peace isn't based on our place in this world, but on our place in God's arms.* Let's not make up worst-case scenarios, but focus on Christ. Holy Spirit is producing the fruit of peace in our lives so we can display Christ's character.

So the next time fear creeps its way in as you respond to God's voice, remember—we can feel uncomfortable but still settle into His arms. Peace comes from God's guaranteed presence, even in painful or chaotic situations. May we trust the peace of Christ to carry us to the places God calls us, even if we feel afraid.

SIMPLE PRAYER

Abba Father, thank You for loving us and sharing Your peace with us. When we're afraid to follow Your will, help us cry out to you with childlike faith. Amen.

DAY 17 HEARING AID: PRAYER

Prayer is one of the greatest ways to focus on Christ and learn to respond to God's voice in a way that honors Him. Begin to thank God for His perfect love, which casts out fear (1 John 4:18).

Ask Holy Spirit to show you where you may be afraid to respond to God's will:

- ◯ fear of failure
- ◯ fear of judgment
- ◯ fear of rejection
- ◯ fear of comparison
- ◯ fear of investing in church community
- ◯ fear of [fill in the blank]

JOURNAL PROMPT

Have you ever allowed your fear to control you in one of these areas? What happened?

Have you ever acted in faith even when you were afraid? What happened?

Don't forget to check off this hearing aid on the contents page after you have completed it.

TIMIDITY

His voice leads us not into timid discipleship but into bold witness.

CHARLES STANLEY

"I walked over to my pastor and said, 'There's a woman over there with crutches, and I feel like the Lord wants me to encourage her that He will heal her,'" Josh said to me casually as our families busily talked around us.

I leaned in to Josh's story, eager for a similar boldness. In fact, that has been my anthem cry for years. Boldness to go places God positioned me to go. Boldness to pursue purpose in a way I didn't fully comprehend. Boldness to speak life into strangers' stories when God was interweaving our paths.

———————————— ○ ————————————

> *Since we have such a hope, we are very bold, not like Moses, who would put a veil over his face so that the Israelites might not gaze at the outcome of what was being brought to an end (2 Corinthians 3:12-13).*

In 2 Corinthians 3, Paul reminds the Corinthians that God qualified them and empowered them to minister. When God gave Moses the law (the old covenant), Moses had to wear a veil to cover the glory that radiated from him after being in God's presence (Exodus 34:33-35). The glory Moses was reflecting was fading. The old covenant, with its laws, traditions, and sacrifices, provided a way to obey God and be blessed. But our standing with God isn't based on our performance or acts. In the new covenant, those saved have already been made holy by the sacrifice of Jesus.

As I was learning to hear God's voice and attempting to walk in confidence, oftentimes I would respond as if I were under the old covenant, thinking if I heard God's voice inviting me to share boldly, then I had to muster the courage to obey. Rather than feeling empowered and qualified by God, I felt all kinds of pressure because I was making it about me. Sometimes I powered through, but often I felt like shrinking back.

As Paul contrasts the old and new covenants, he shows that we can be bold in the new covenant and the hope found in Jesus. We have a lasting confidence. Paul goes on to say,

> *Now the Lord is the Spirit, and where the Spirit of the Lord is, there is freedom. And we all, with unveiled face, beholding the glory of the Lord, are being transformed into the same image from one degree of glory to another. For this comes from the Lord who is the Spirit (2 Corinthians 3:17-18).*

Holy Spirit empowers you to reflect the majesty of the Lord!

———————— ○ ————————

So what happened to the lady with the crutches? There was Josh in a church service, wondering if the Lord really was about to heal this lady. He felt a sense of nervous excitement as he wondered if he was just being crazy or if he should go encourage her with what he felt the Lord shared with him. Holy Spirit filled him with supernatural courage. Heart pounding, he walked over to his pastor and told him what he was feeling.

His pastor guided him with a few questions. "Have you talked to the woman about it?" Within a few minutes and with his pastor's go-ahead, Josh walked over to the woman. He didn't pull a "thus says the Lord." Rather, he simply explained what he felt the Lord put on his heart.

Her faith was stirred, and she discerned that the Lord was indeed encouraging her through Josh. Moments later, God healed that woman. This private exchange became public as everyone in the room was filled with faith and others began experiencing healing too.

That woman left the service without the crutches, and the church witnessed God's miraculous power that day. What I love about this moment is that Holy Spirit invited Josh to be a part of the miracle and fueled him with supernatural boldness, and he was able to recognize it.

The ability to hear God in the heat of the moment is developed by listening to God in daily disciplines of silence, prayer, studying and meditating on His Word, and worship. But here's the thing: If we're looking for God only in the big things, we miss Him in the everyday. It's in the day-to-day moments of meeting with God that we begin to reflect what we behold.

We already inherited boldness as part of our relationship with Jesus. Are we able to recognize it?

Josh doesn't come from a lineage of healing evangelists who demonstrated God's power in this way. He's a man who remains humble and recognizes God's voice because he spends time with Him. Just as he modeled, we overcome our timidity by boldly depending on Christ. We no longer operate out of written law, but the Spirit. Walking in the boldness He provides makes our faith exciting, demonstrates the power of Jesus, and leaves a lasting impact. You too can walk boldly and be free from that crutch of timidity!

DAY 18 HEARING AID: PEOPLE

In chapter 7, we considered the way God speaks through people. Today He's going to speak through you. Now that you aren't focusing on your own timidity but on the boldness you have in Christ, spend a few moments in prayer, asking God to put a person on your heart. Maybe it's your coworker, family member, fellow worshipper, bestie…

Now ask Holy Spirit what He might have you say to that person.

JOURNAL PROMPT

Who is the person?

What helpful words is Holy Spirit inviting you to share with that person?

Do these words encourage, comfort, or strengthen that person?

o *Yes.*   o *No. (Try again.)* ↑

Does God want you to share these words today with that person?

o *Yes.*   o *No.*

Write a card, drop a text, or message them boldly! Don't shrink back out of fear, but embrace how God is leading. You might start with, "Hey, I was praying for you today and I felt…"

Don't pretend He answered no just because you're too scared to share. God may invite you to share with that person later. Or sometimes God puts someone on your heart so you can pray for them. Pray boldly for that person right now.

19

SUFFERING

Just as Jesus learned obedience by the things He suffered,
we learn obedience by the difficult circumstances we face.
When we obey the Word of God that is spoken by the Holy Spirit,
we will grow and mature in the times of conflict and suffering.

JOHN BEVERE

We're still in act 2 of *Getting to Know God's Voice*, processing through some common holdups and hang-ups that hinder us from hearing Him.

The Bible actually talks about how we're going to suffer and endure trials. I mean, wouldn't it be great if Christianity was made up of lollipops, unicorns, and rainbows all the time? But since we want to keep it real, let's talk about the complexities of suffering and our response as believers. This chapter is focusing on suffering that *isn't* the result of our poor life choices or disobedience.

We're discussing the unexplainable, potentially soul-crushing suffering that is associated with the fall and brokenness of humanity. The suffering that's hard to wrap your head around, doesn't make sense, and may make you want to ice out God.

———————————— ○ ————————————

Ultimate Utopia was a faith-based TV show I produced for a local television station when I was in college. We often featured a "person on the street" segment in which we asked people in the community some thought-provoking questions. One interview is forever etched in my mind.

The host of the show, Mike, spotted a gray-haired man with a kind smile across the street. We lugged the camera, tripod, and mic over to this man and struck up a casual conversation. When Mike asked if we could interview him and shared the topic, the man had a resigned look in his eyes, but he moved forward with the interview anyway.

"Rolling!" I said as I positioned the camera on top of my shoulder. I zoomed in to a medium shot to show the top of the man's dirt-covered jeans, white T-shirt, and ruffled hair.

"Do you attend church?" Mike asked as he pointed the mic toward him.

Blinking back tears, he responded, "I used to be a pastor but left the church. My daughter died, and I've been mad at God ever since."

I briefly caught a glimpse of his aching heart, desperate for resolution. I wanted answers. I wanted to know why a man who had dedicated his life to serving the local church lost one of the most important things in his life. I wanted to figure out a way to rationalize the suffering. I, too, wondered where God was when the man's daughter died.

I can't remember how our conversation ended. I wish we had hugged it out or I had boldly told the man with the kind smile, "God can handle your anger, your grief, your sorrow. Let Him be your Father in this pain."

As I heard the former pastor with the kind smile share about his anger and the rejection he felt toward God, I saw that suffering doesn't separate us from hearing God; our unhealthy response to suffering does. We isolate ourselves from God because of the deep complexities He hasn't untangled, the questions He has yet to answer, and the agonizing outcomes we experience.

We must remember that we don't know the eternal outcome. Jesus did provide a resolution to our suffering. He took our despair and sorrow on Himself and entered into suffering for us on the cross. Jesus's temporary suffering ended our eternal suffering.

Maybe you gave up trying to hear God's voice because you can't figure out why your mom was in so much pain that she committed suicide. Or maybe you're struggling to rationalize why you can't hold down a job. Maybe your suffering is caused by a disease that invaded your body.

What if instead of crying out for an answer, we cried out for our Creator? Perhaps if we could let go of seeking an answer for our suffering, we will be more likely to see our Savior. When profound pain shakes the foundations of our faith, we must hold on to the truth that Holy Spirit is not the antagonist we run from, but our advocate we run to. In the pain of losing a mother, God is close by, carrying comfort. In the suffering of losing a job, God provides peace in our uncertainty. In the health what-ifs, God assures us that He will restore our broken bodies (whether on this side of eternity or not).

SUFFERING DOESN'T SEPARATE US FROM GOD; OUR UNHEALTHY RESPONSE TO SUFFERING DOES.

You are not meant to bear the weight of the cross the way Christ does. His life, death, and resurrection give us space to see the miracle of who He is. Your heavy heart doesn't diminish God's holiness on the earth. God is still holy, right there in the middle of your hard, horribly unjust, or unbearable circumstance. Being a follower of Christ doesn't make you immune to suffering; it just helps you remain attuned and comforted by the presence of God in the middle of affliction. Rather than running from God when we hurt, may we run toward Him.

Your story does not end in the suffering. Hold on to this truth:

> *After you have suffered a little while, the God of all grace, who has called you to his eternal glory in Christ, will himself restore, confirm, strengthen, and establish you. To him be the dominion forever and ever. Amen (1 Peter 5:10-11).*

SIMPLE PRAYER

Lord, please open our eyes to see Your goodness

in the middle of suffering. May we run toward Your

presence for comfort, strength, and peace.

Amen.

DAY 19 HEARING AID: CIRCUMSTANCES

If you've gone through deep suffering or sorrow, let's create space for you to process it. The last thing I want to do is minimize your trials or heartache. Jesus brings spiritual resolution and can provide practical helps for walking through this healing process. Prayerfully ask Holy Spirit…

- O to give you wisdom to see the goodness of God amid your pain
- O to show you the next step to healing

JOURNAL PROMPT

Has a painful circumstance tempted you to isolate yourself from God or question His goodness?

What next step might God be inviting you to take? Is it counseling? Seeking guidance from a trusted pastor? Prayer with a friend?

20

NEGLECTING
THE GIFTS

The Spirit-filled life is not a special, deluxe edition of Christianity.
It is part and parcel of the total plan of God for His people.

A.W. TOZER

My daughter, Zoey, tiptoed into my office as I ended my workday. She placed a special gift in front of me. I saw the glue on her fingers and feather pieces stuck to her shirt. It was abstract art made of large teal, purple, yellow, and orange feathers placed on a rectangle cardboard piece.

There she was, expressing her heart through this beautiful gift. How awful would it be if I didn't hold out my hand to accept it? Could you imagine her standing there and me just looking away, not even acknowledging her presence?

Could you imagine us doing that to Holy Spirit?

The second Jesus came into your life and saved you, He gave you Holy Spirit. Holy Spirit gives you gifts, not based on your natural giftedness but because of His grace. His supernatural gifts aren't just for you; rather, they demonstrate the truth, power, and love of Jesus through you.

There are different kinds of gifts, but the same Spirit distributes them. There are different kinds of service, but the same Lord. There are different kinds of working, but in all of them and in everyone it is the same God at work.

Now to each one the manifestation of the Spirit is given for the common good. To one there is given through the Spirit a message of wisdom, to another a message of knowledge by means of the same Spirit, to another faith by the same Spirit, to another gifts of healing by that one Spirit, to another miraculous powers, to another prophecy, to another distinguishing between spirits, to another speaking in different kinds of tongues, and to still another the interpretation of tongues. All these are the work of one and the same Spirit, and he distributes them to each one, just as he determines (1 Corinthians 12:4-11 NIV).

The Bible mentions many more gifts, including mercy, teaching, evangelism, apostleship, craftsmanship, administration, and so on. You can also find spiritual gift assessment tests online. If you take one, please make sure it includes the gifts mentioned in 1 Corinthains 12:4-11. These are often referred to as power, revelatory, or supernatural gifts because of the way they display God's power.

Holy Spirit gifts are for the common good of the church, even if they're demonstrated outside church walls. And they should always point people to Christ. One gift may be more prevalent in your life, but because *For example, we don't heal people; Jesus does.* you have an all-access pass to the gift-giver, God can work through you in various ways when necessary.

At a prayer meeting I attended, Holy Spirit helped me recognize that a person in the group was being deceitful and was deeply troubled in his soul. He requested prayer for his parents because he felt they were acting unjustly. I began to feel unsettled—something was off with this man's request. As we prayed, I sensed anger taking root in his life. God empowered me to pray life-giving words into this young man's journey. Other church members spoke encouraging words to him as well.

After our prayer time closed, this man shared that he had thoughts of severely harming his parents and wishing them dead. Later, a pastor came alongside him and helped him get the additional care he needed. Crisis averted—and it all started with God alerting us to the real situation.

In chapter 7, I mentioned that I usually run away from dramatic situations like that. It is *not* my go-to response to call out evil and stand up to forces of *I get squeamish even typing that.* darkness. When you walk in the power of Holy Spirit, He empowers you in ways you might not expect, using super-natural gifts to strengthen the kingdom. *That is enough to get some Holy Spirit gumption all up in this place!*

Let's go back to my daughter's feather art for a second. I placed this gift next to another gift Zoey had given my husband. It was a small birdhouse painted with the same colors. When I placed them beside each other, I noticed how complementary they were even though they had different functions.

We are given different spiritual gifts that function together to build the body of Christ, just as the prayer story demonstrated. Multiple gifts were active as we prayed for that man. As the church functions the way God intended, a beautiful interdependency and cohesiveness builds it into the image of Christ.

Hear me when I yell this all up in your face—*I am not suggesting we interrupt the Sunday sermon in a heavenly language as one pew neighbor casts out demons and someone else performs a miracle of healing over the first-time visitor in the arm sling.* Pastors and other church leaders need to gently teach people how to use their God-given gifts in a relationally appropriate way that honors God and other people. ← *Perhaps you've seen your share of crazy.*

God is a God of order, and there is a healthy way for gifts to operate in church services or in small groups. So let's not ignore Holy Spirit or neglect His gifts just because they have been abused.

What would it look like if we received the gifts with eager availability and open hands to serve and love? When the gifts operate in unity, community is built. If you are interested in learning how the supernatural gifts operate in your local church, please continue the discussion with your church leaders.

And remember, as you exercise the gifts Holy Spirit gives you, always prayerfully consider, *Is this gift operating according to the character of Christ and the Word of God?* Using your gifts in that framework will help others experience His kingdom on earth.

Honor Holy Spirit by valuing the gifts He's given you. Support others as they learn to use their gifts, and give God the glory as He does awesome things.

WHEN THE GIFTS OPERATE IN UNITY, COMMUNITY IS BUILT. HONOR HOLY SPIRIT BY PLACING VALUE ON THE GIFTS HE'S GIVEN YOU.

DAY 20 HEARING AID: CREATION

Spend time today connecting to our Creator in nature. Go for a walk, jump in some waves, or watch the sunset and reflect on the awe-inspiring power of our loving God. If you're unable to go outside, adapt this challenge to fit your needs.

Ask this same awesome Creator to empower you to receive your Holy Spirit gifts with a fresh excitement.

JOURNAL PROMPT

Describe a time you saw someone exercise a powerful Holy Spirit gift in a healthy way.

Describe a time when you sensed that Holy Spirit was working through you.

21

HOW IS HOLY SPIRIT WORKING IN YOU?

Congrats on making it through act 2 and taking time to think through the holdups and hang-ups that could hinder Holy Spirit's activity in your life. Check in with your accountability partner and send them all the high-fives for making it this far.

o *Did it!*   o *Nah, I'm lazy.*

You had your warrior gear on and leaned into God's voice as we talked about freedom from sin, shame, and unhealthy beliefs that may have been hindering your walk with Him. Holy Spirit manifests supernatural gifts *through* your life, not because of your character, but because of His power. The fruit of the Spirit is the character and nature of Jesus that is displayed *in* your life.

> HOLY SPIRIT MANIFESTS SUPERNATURAL GIFTS THROUGH YOU, NOT BECAUSE OF YOUR CHARACTER, BUT BECAUSE OF HIS POWER.

> *The fruit of the Spirit is love, joy, peace, patience, kindness, goodness, faithfulness, gentleness, self-control; against such things there is no law. And those who belong to Christ Jesus have crucified the flesh with its passions and desires (Galatians 5:22-24).*

Pause for a minute and reflect: When have you noticed spiritual fruit developing in your life?

If you find that your attitude and actions aren't displaying the fruit of the Spirit, prayerfully review act 2 and invite Holy Spirit to highlight anything you need to spend more time on. Galatians 5:25 reminds us, "If we live by the Spirit, let us also keep in step with the Spirit."

Remember these key reminders from act 2 as you keep in step with the Spirit:

- Remain confident in Christ instead of yourself.
- When Holy Spirit lives in you, sin does not get to control you.
- Be comfortable in the waiting.
- Honor Holy Spirit by placing value on the gifts He's given you.
- God is inviting you into community (the church).
- Peace comes from the guaranteed presence of God.
- Boldly depend on Christ.
- Holy Spirit is not the antagonist in your suffering; He is the advocate you can run to.
- Gifts operating in unity build community.

DAY 21 HEARING AID: FREESTYLE

Take some extra time with God today. Whether through prayer, worship, or studying God's Word, ask Him to speak to you about a specific circumstance in your life. Trust that God will respond.

JOURNAL PROMPT

What might God be saying to you today?

Share what you heard with a leader, accountability partner, or family member. After you do, don't forget to check off this hearing aid on the contents page.

GOD'S PURPOSE RELEASES
HIS POWER AND PROMISES,
CREATING NEW POSSIBILITIES.

ACT 3

OVERFLOWING WITH POSSIBILITY AND PROMISE

Lord, may Your Spirit spill from our lives so we overflow with Your possibility and promise.

22

INTRODUCTION TO ACT 3

Trying to do the Lord's work in your own strength is the most confusing, exhausting, and tedious of all work. But when you are filled with the Holy Spirit, then the ministry of Jesus just flows out of you.

CORRIE TEN BOOM

> Human anger does not produce the righteousness God desires. So get rid of all the filth and evil in your lives, and humbly accept the word God has planted in your hearts, for it has the power to save your souls.
>
> But don't just listen to God's word. You must do what it says. Otherwise, you are only fooling yourselves. For if you listen to the word and don't obey, it is like glancing at your face in a mirror. You see yourself, walk away, and forget what you look like. But if you look carefully into the perfect law that sets you free, and if you do what it says and don't forget what you heard, then God will bless you for doing it (James 1:20-25 NLT).

Don't be the man in the mirror. Just as James highlights in the passage above, we study the Word of God and discern God's voice through it…and then we must also carry it out. People who hear the Word but focus only on themselves will walk away, forget who they are, and disobey. They become deceived. But people who look at the Word carefully and remember to center their lives on Christ will act in obedience and be blessed.

Today matters. It's the day your joy-filled smile brightens someone's heartache. Or the day the just-because text you send a weary dad helps him see the peace he brings his family. Today matters as you spend time developing spiritual disciplines, like studying your Bible, praying, and worshipping Jesus. These small acts produce a solid faith and build the strength you need when facing the "bigger" moments God leads you through. Your obedience matters as you build a relationship with a new friend by saying hi to them at the library. It matters as you pray like a mama bear and ask God to free your troubled teen from addiction. It matters when you fumble your way through an encouraging word that confirms a goal your pastor has but hasn't yet shared publicly.

GOD'S PURPOSE RELEASES HIS POWER AND PROMISES, CREATING NEW POSSIBILITIES.

Influence is a by-product of serving and walking in obedience to Christ. As you follow Christ, you lead in His strength and recognize opportunities to see God's good even in the bad, you speak words of life instead of death, you respond with hope instead of horror, and you trust that God is moving just as His Word says He is. Your obedience today sets up your opportunities tomorrow and the next day and the next. From the seemingly mundane moments to the shout-it-from-the-rooftop miracles, following God's purpose releases His power and promises, creating new possibilities.

You're ready to step into greater obedience. In act 1 of this book, we learned that God has countless ways to communicate with us. We also built a healthy perspective on the ways God speaks. His spoken word does not contradict the written Word or His character. We considered the way God speaks through Holy Spirit, Jesus, the Bible, church, worship, circumstances, people, prayer, a small voice inside us, and creation.

In act 2, we made ourselves available for God to heal us of spiritual deafness and free us from setbacks. We also understand we can't create a miracle by praying a certain way. We let God be God and realize His ways are sometimes beyond our ability to understand. We get to fight against a complacent faith with humble action. Now that we have ears to hear and eyes to see, we get to see Holy Spirit minister through us as we take action. We already have the framework to walk boldly wherever God leads. Let's march on in act 3 and embrace adventures with God.

The hearing aids in the rest of the book will challenge you to connect with others and encourage them. As God carries out His plan, get ready to be mobilized for mission. In this final section, trust that Holy Spirit will fill you to overflowing and spill out of you in new and powerful ways.

SIMPLE PRAYER

Lord, may we step courageously

into the areas You've prepared

our hearts to explore.

Amen.

DAY 22 HEARING AID: QUIET TIME

In today's challenge, you'll experiment with quieting your mind and freeing yourself from distractions during one interaction. Whether you are dropping the kids off at school, grocery shopping, working, participating in a Bible study, or making dinner with a friend, intentionally silence the external ruckus so you won't be distracted from God's voice in the situation. For example, when I've chosen a time to do this, I put away my phone because I'm easily distracted by it.

When is the window in your day when will you try this? Who will you be with?

Ask Holy Spirit if you can partner with Him on anything. From a simple smile to the barista to striking up a convo with a stranger, show up for it!

Disclaimers:

○ Remember guidelines on page 11 and be relationally appropriate. People aren't projects—they are humans with tender hearts, just like you and me.

○ When God invites you to be a part of His divine story in someone's life, He may be speaking to you just as much as He is to them. Listen and learn.

○ If God invites you to speak with a stranger, please be smart and safe!

Did you find yourself getting distracted?

What steps can you take to create a distraction-free zone next time?

Did your interaction with the person seem any different from usual?

23

FAITH-FUELED OBEDIENCE

It is never a question of how much you and I have of the Spirit,
but how much He has of us.

BILLY GRAHAM

> *Therefore, preparing your minds for action, and being*
> *sober-minded, set your hope fully on the grace that will*
> *be brought to you at the revelation of Jesus Christ. As*
> *obedient children, do not be conformed to the passions*
> *of your former ignorance, but as he who called you is holy,*
> *you also be holy in all your conduct, since it is written,*
> *"You shall be holy, for I am holy" (1 Peter 1:13-16).*

At a young age, my friend Jeremy, now a Hollywood screenwriter and producer, felt called to influence the entertainment industry. In one of his first jobs in the business, he worked for a producer who was an atheist. As they worked side by side, Jeremy learned that the producer was estranged from his son.

One day Jeremy had one of those Holy Spirit nudges. You know…a random thought turns into a holy prompting that you just can't let go of. Jeremy leaned in a little closer to this God-moment and sensed God inviting him to help repair this broken father-son relationship. Holy Spirit began to show Jeremy what that would look like, the materials he needed, and when it had to happen.

Would you obey in this moment?

○ *Yes!*　　　　　　　　　○ *No way!*

When God invites us to risk boldly, we face so many unknowns. Would Jeremy's boss laugh in his face and call him "Jesus boy," as he had done before? Would Jeremy lean in, listen, and respond to an opportunity that could threaten the career he felt called to pursue?

Jeremy knew what might happen if he said yes to something without knowing the outcome. But isn't that what obedience is? Obedience powered by Holy Spirit is a faith walk of trusting in a God who actually knows the outcome.

Jeremy drove to the producer's house, responding to the prompting of a life-giving God instead of his own doubts and the potential fallout. Sitting in his car, sweaty and nauseous, he passionately pleaded with God, telling Him that he really didn't want to do this.

OBEDIENCE POWERED BY HOLY SPIRIT IS A FAITH WALK OF TRUSTING IN A GOD WHO ACTUALLY KNOWS WHAT HE'S TALKING ABOUT.

As children of God, we get to play a role in something far greater than we can fully comprehend. Father God invites us to be Jesus's hands and feet by participating in His work on earth. Holy Spirit speaks; we get to respond. Our response could be a wink from heaven to another person that says, "You're seen, known, and loved."

Nervously, Jeremy got out of his car with a stack of envelopes wrapped in a bow. He had written the estranged son's address on all the envelopes and stamped each one. Jeremy placed the envelopes by the door and did a "doorbell-ditch." The thought of waiting around to see the producer's response was just too much, so Jeremy did what many of us would do in this situation. He ran away.

That night Jeremy and his boss attended a party for a movie they were both working on. The moment his boss and his boss's wife locked eyes with Jeremy, they began to weep. As they approached Jeremy, the man said, "We were in the house talking, and I said to my wife, 'I really need to do something about communicating with my son. I need to figure out what to do.'"

His wife had responded, "You should write letters."

Ding-dong.

The stack of envelopes on their porch shook them to the core. In time, Jeremy's boss faithfully used all the envelopes...and more. In a divinely orchestrated moment this family will never forget, God used Jeremy's obedience to strengthen them to love fully.

Like Jeremy, we get to respond to God's promptings in our day-to-day activities and make room for His love and promise in our circumstances. Obedience is a character trait in God's family. My prayer is that we won't don't miss it. As Peter declared in Acts 11:17 (TPT), "Who am I to stand in the way?"

SIMPLE PRAYER

Lord, may we listen

attentively and respond

accordingly as You move!

Amen.

DAY 23 HEARING AID: CHURCH

Write an encouraging card to your pastor or another leader at church. Prayerfully consider with Holy Spirit how God sees that person. Let go of your own agenda, and practice seeing them the way God does. In your note, share that description and thank them for serving and strengthening the church. It doesn't have to be fancy—just sincere!

JOURNAL PROMPT

Who will you write the note to?

What does God think about them?

Are these thoughts encouraging and comforting? If so, get the church's mailing address and send your note. If not, try again!

Don't forget to check off this challenge on the contents page after you complete it.

24

HOPE AND JOY

*Simply by our proximity to Jesus, we can bring hope and life to
people and places trapped in discouragement and despair.*

LOUIE GIGLIO

"Be expectant!"

I raised my hand, positioned to propel my phone across the room. Instead I settled for an uber-dramatic eye roll at my friend on the other end of the phone call. To me, it was such an overused, fast-pass one-liner that has become diluted of meaning.

Expectancy carries promise for the future or pain from the past. I was responding from the pain in my past.

> *May the God of hope fill you with all joy and peace in believing, so that by the power of the Holy Spirit you may abound in hope (Romans 15:13).*

FUN FACT

Romans 15:13 is a benediction Paul wrote in a letter to the church in Rome—Jews and Gentiles joined together in a new community. The letter highlights the relationships between weak and strong believers. This blessing sums up themes in the entire letter.

You can find hope and joy in...

- ◯ your connection to other people (temporary hope)
- ◯ your connection to stuff or circumstance (temporary hope)
- ◯ your connection to Christ (eternal hope)

The World Yells About Our Pain from the Past

It's ironic, really. We're sometimes told to be expectant in general but not to hope for specific outcomes because that can lead to disappointment. Expectancy can be a painful reminder of the times we got hurt in relationships. Disappointment and bitterness can develop when relationships don't go the way we imagined they would.

You expect your bestie to call you on your birthday, but she forgets. You ice her out rather than talking to her about your hurt.

You expect to be a parent and harden your heart toward God when it doesn't happen the way you imagine.

You anticipated a job promotion but got a pink slip instead, and you feel pain and anger for years.

But our eternal God is a God of hope in the past, present, and future! A mature faith is expectant and carries healthy expectations for us and others in Christ.

The Lord Reminds Us of His Promise for the Future

The expectancy my friend was referring to on the phone wasn't based on human abilities, but on Christ's. Our expectancy carries promise. The great thing in hearing God's voice is that in the Bible, He clearly tells us what we can expect from Him. As we see the truth through the ← *This is why it's so valuable to study the Word!*

lens of promise, joy is produced. God is who He says He is. As Romans 15:13 says, we abound in hope.

As you face thyroid disease, the promise of a resurrected body fills you with expectancy, and you overflow with hope.

You feel lonely, but you remember that the Lord will never leave you or forsake you.

Your child struggles with being bullied at school, but you carry promise that God loves him even more than you do, and you help your child take healthy steps with hope.

We have all we need. Enough to navigate relational conflict, financial difficulties, and health issues. Enough to see victory. From this place of hope in Christ and the expectancy of future restoration, we overflow with an abundance of joy.

———————————— ○ ————————————

Recently I visited a third world country and was deeply inspired by a woman I met there. She demonstrated a mature faith in the face of extreme poverty. She understood how to hold pain and joy in the same breath. I couldn't help but notice how much stuff she *didn't* have, but she didn't see her life that way. In Christ she found security and opportunity for expectancy. Her circumstances didn't derail her joy or hope. We can all learn from her example!

How often have we let even the littlest setbacks dictate our attitude? Has your joy ever been sucked out of your job, or your role as a parent, or a friendship, or your day-to-day activities? Remember, this joy the Bible speaks of is the fruit of Holy Spirit. It's easy to be distracted from God's voice. It takes discipline to be fruitful. Be intentional about maintaining a sense of expectancy by studying the Word and abiding in Christ. From that place, there's joy and hope.

Your Cup Overflows

Imagine a giant coffee mug filled to the brim with the fanciest coffee ever. As you carry your mug, someone bumps into you. What spills out? Is it confetti? Milk? Tea? Diet Pepsi? Obviously not. Your cup is filled with magic coffee, so that's what spills out. Others could even smell, see, and taste your coffee if they really wanted to.

HOLY SPIRIT FILLS YOU WITH JOY AND HOPE THAT OTHERS FIND CONTAGIOUS.

When you are bumped or rattled by life, do you spill out a grumpy attitude, worry, anger, stress, or fear? Or are joy, hope, and expectancy splashing all over the place? As you spill out joy, what you're really saying is, "Taste and see that the Lord is good." As you trust in Jesus and live with expectancy for the future, He fills you with joy and peace. As a man or woman of joy, you carry expectancy through God's promise and His resurrection power. Have expectancy, friend. Holy Spirit fills you with joy and hope that others find contagious. They'll notice just how different you are as you stand out for Him.

SIMPLE PRAYER

Holy Spirit, may we respond in expectancy with the hope we have in You. Fill us with overflowing joy! Amen.

DAY 24 HEARING AID: PEOPLE

Today's hearing aid challenge will be a confetti-to-the-face situation. Think of a friend or family member who could use a little joy. Ask Holy Spirit how you can overflow with His joy in order to be a mouthpiece of Jesus today. Maybe it's leaving cookies at their desk or showing up at their house and literally throwing confetti at their face (and cleaning it up afterward—ha!). Joy may not fix their situation, but you're demonstrating the love of Jesus, and that speaks loud enough.

JOURNAL PROMPT

Who will you reach out to today?

After you do, write in your journal about what happened.

After you complete this hearing aid, check it off on the contents page.

25

GUIDANCE

Lord, use me today, use me for your glory, make me bold, stir me up,
give me eyes to see the needs of those I work with, give me a heart
sensitive to those who are hurting, give me a prompting of the
Spirit to minister to those who are around me.

CRAIG GROESCHEL

"Wait, what did you want again?" he asked with a confused smile.

Matt, our kids, and I hit up a donut shop after church. The man behind the counter with tattoo-covered arms—let's call him Donut Devan—maintained his fun-loving attitude as I placed a semi-complicated order for coffee and mass quantities of donuts. I was instantly drawn to him. He was kindhearted and professional and knew how to be playfully outspoken without being offensive.

"Nah, you won't want that pumpkin drink. Try this one—I made three this morning and didn't mess it up!" He carried a rare confidence.

After making my drink, he brought it to us, made himself comfortable at the table next to ours, and leaned in to chat. Hearing we were new in town, he told us about the best beaches, attractions our kids may like, and how much he loves the local NFL team. As Matt and I continued to chat with him, I felt a nudge to affirm his father heart. I didn't spend hours in prayer or seek wise counsel about this. I just sensed that still, small voice in my spirit guiding me to affirm another person.

Donut Devan was built like a linebacker. He looked young and wasn't rocking dad jeans or a wedding ring. I couldn't see anything that confirmed he was a dad. The convo continued, and I casually asked, "Do you have kids?"

That simple question opened up his story. "I have three. Two live here with their mom, and the other one lives on the other side of the country. They just spent the whole summer with me. Burned my pockets dry," he laughed.

"You need a nap! You seem so kind and caring; I'm sure you're an amazing father." I looked directly into his eyes and prayed those words would stick.

The conversation continued as he shared the relational hardships he faced and what it was like being in his kids' lives. "My then-girlfriend left with my son when he was two, and now he's ten. I just saw him for the first time since they left, and it's like we haven't missed a beat."

Matt spoke up warmly, "You guys will always have that special connection. You're his father." One strong father upheld another, and it seemed like the moment of affirmation Devan's spirit needed.

We talked about God and the church. He mentioned that he attends occasionally but still struggles in some areas, and he shared his dream of owning a business someday. Our ten-minute convo didn't end with a dramatic conversion. In between donut bits, we didn't pray for healing in his family or for financial blessing in his future business. We would have if we felt the Lord was inviting us to do that, but for today, we simply sat together, listened to each other, and saw one another.

As you hear Holy Spirit using your actions and words to affirm and encourage others, His resurrection power is released. In the Gospels, Jesus sends out his 12 apostles as missionaries. He gives them authority to do the same work He has been doing—casting out demons, healing diseases, raising the dead, and proclaiming the kingdom of heaven (Matthew 10:1-15). He also warns them they will be persecuted for their faith (verses 15-18). Then he adds this promise:

> *Do not be anxious how you are to speak or what you are*
> *to say, for what you are to say will be given to you in that*
> *hour. For it is not you who speak, but the Spirit of your*
> *Father speaking through you (verses 19-20).*

What would happen if we followed the apostles' example and maintained their tenacity, leaning into the guidance of Holy Spirit and trusting that He is guiding and speaking through us? As we follow Jesus in our trials and (donut) triumphs, God does not forsake us. His Spirit will always be with us and speak through us.

Do you trust God's guidance enough to open your mouth? That day with Donut Devan, we simply affirmed him as a father. We would have missed Devan's joy, his vision for the future, and his passion for people if we had stayed hyper-focused on donuts and coffee. I think we all felt the significance of our paths intervening that Sunday.

Don't miss out on God's mission for you; even the small stuff carries significance. Trust Holy Spirit to speak through you. It may bless you as much as it blesses others.

SIMPLE PRAYER

Jesus, may we be people who cooperate
with You as You transform lives. Thank You
for guiding us; we trust You fully and glorify
You wholeheartedly.

Amen.

DAY 25 HEARING AID: JESUS

Ask the Lord for guidance, and then phone a friend or family member just to say hello. (No fair texting!) During the conversation, be sensitive to Holy Spirit's guidance to ask questions or bring up topics. There's no need to "thus says the Lord" anything. Just trust His leading and see what happens.

JOURNAL PROMPT

Who did you call?

How did it go? Did you feel prompted to ask any questions or bring up any topics? If so, what were they?

If not, how might Holy Spirit have used your obedience anyway?

After you take action and reflect on how this went, check off this challenge on the contents page.

26

UNITY

Unity does not mean sameness.
It means oneness of purpose.

PRISCILLA SHIRER

What would happen if a church devolved into a culture of bullying, self-serving, divisiveness, or simply unresponsiveness? How would a church of consumers be different from a church that champions what God wants? Here's one way to think about it.

Have you ever seen privacy glass at a fancy hotel? With the flick of a switch, the glass becomes either transparent or completely opaque. When the electric current is on, certain molecules are aligned between panels, and light passes through. When the current is off, those molecules fall out of alignment, blocking the light. The voltage is always available, but it isn't always activated.

Shout me down with those "hallelujahs" as I full-circle this moment. When churches operate in "off" mode, the members are out of step with one another and their mission. But when the members access Holy Spirit's power, everything changes. The members are aligned, and God's light shines through.

In the engineering world, another word for "voltage" is "potential." In the privacy glass, as the potential is recognized, the molecules become unified, and the glass fulfills its purpose.

Let's segue from engineering to the Bible. The apostle Paul encourages everyone—in his context, Jews and Gentiles—to live in the unity and peace Jesus provided. As we do, our oneness and unity empower us to fulfill our mission. When we become united in our mission, we reach our potential and fulfill our purpose.

Colossians 1:10

> *I therefore, a prisoner for the Lord, urge you to* walk *in a manner worthy of the calling to which you have been called, with all humility and gentleness, with patience, bearing with one another in love, eager to maintain the unity of the Spirit in the bond of peace. There is one body and one Spirit—just as you were called to the one hope that belongs to your call—one Lord, one faith, one baptism, one God and Father of all, who is over all and through all and in all (Ephesians 4:1-6).*

When we activate Holy Spirit's power in these three areas, we experience unity:

① declaring in faith that Jesus is over all

② relying on Holy Spirit to develop our character (the fruit of the Spirit)

③ using the gifts God has given us

When Holy Spirit moves freely in our lives and our churches, we experience miraculous unity. In our churches, we can help maintain unity by praying for our leaders, demonstrating self-control by arriving on time for service, holding our tongue when we want to criticize the sermon, humbly serving where we are needed, and obediently and boldly utilizing our spiritual gifts. Imagine what would happen if we all walked as the image-bearers of Christ we're designed to be!

Unity does not mean uniformity. We must appreciate our spiritual sisters' and brothers' diverse gifts, talents, and abilities. In the unity of Holy Spirit, we can champion the vision of the church, and our faith can mature.

When we don't flip the power switch on, we act out of order. We get scattered and chaotic, and the gospel is dimly lit. We make decisions according to popular demand rather than biblical doctrine. We use our gifts to perform for God and other people rather than letting them flow from the peace we have been given.

WHEN HOLY SPIRIT MOVES FREELY IN OUR LIVES AND OUR CHURCHES, WE EXPERIENCE MIRACULOUS UNITY

On the other hand, when we access Holy Spirit's power, we are united as members of one body. We have different functions but a common purpose. We are on the same mission—to bring Christ glory. A united church is a safe space to work for social justice, allow the gifts to operate, discover the character of Christ, and point people to His love and promises. A united church weeps over the things that break God's heart, speaks words of life into dead and broken situations, and boldly prays for Christ to heal even in seemingly hopeless conditions. A church that rests in God's sovereignty while awakened to heaven's perspective will change the landscape of a city. Our light will no longer be darkened. We'll shine bright in our church communities, spreading His light into our workplaces, families, and schools.

SIMPLE PRAYER
Lord, help us celebrate our local church, support our leaders, and maintain our unity through Jesus.
Amen.

DAY 26 HEARING AID: PRAYER

Take some time with God to pray about and reflect on these points:

How can you actively promote unity in your church relationships?

Ask God to show you ways you can serve in your local church. Then connect with a church leader and see if there's a spot to serve in that way. If not, consider serving in an area of need.

Pray for your church and its leaders. If you feel like God is giving you an encouraging word for your church, share it with a church leader. Not sure how to pray? Check out Romans 8:26.

JOURNAL PROMPT

Record some ideas that came to mind in your prayer time. Steps for promoting unity in your relationships, ways to serve, encouraging words to share…

When you've completed this hearing aid, remember to check it off on the contents page.

27

REVELATION

As God's children, we are not to be observers; we're to participate actively in the Lord's work. Spectators sit and watch, but we are called to use our spiritual gifts and serve continually.

CHARLES STANLEY

Have you ever been in a workout, listening to praise and worship music, and totally tuned out the gym around you? Rocking on the elliptical hidden in the back of the gym, I was in that zone. Hot and smelly, all-in with praise hands in the air, doing a fake stretch kinda thing. My legs were screaming to stop, but God was saying let's go.

I saw a stranger four rows in front of me, and I instantly felt like the Lord invited me to go talk to him. The problem was, that's scary. What was I supposed to do, offer high-fives and water squirts to the face? I reminded God I was an introvert and bullet-pointed all the reasons I couldn't do this.

- ○ I didn't want to be *that* crazy girl.

- ○ It was awkward.

- ○ I didn't have the guts to walk four rows in front of all the other people...and possibly say something stupid.

He must have forgotten.

161

How would you respond?

O Run away and save face.   o Obey and potentially look a little cray-cray.

God played the God card and reminded me about the theme of my prayers lately. I wanted to step into greater boldness, and this was an opportunity for that. He reminded me of Joshua 1:9 (NIV): "Be strong and courageous...for the Lord your God will be with you wherever you go." Would I trust Him?

As I continued to work out, I repented and thanked Him for teaching me who He is. And since fear is *not* a spiritual gift, I took a step forward, trusting that Holy Spirit was wanting to operate through me.

God, I'll do it...and then I set up some stipulations. *But I have 20 minutes left in my workout.*

Stranger Dude was on the machine four rows in front of me, and the exit was off to the right. So I threw out a fleece (we talked about that on day 6). If he randomly ended up in the back row, then game on.

I actually try not to do this, so whoops.

As I continued to work out, I realized I had no idea what I was supposed to say to this man. I continued to pray and arm-stretch-worship, and as I did, I felt like God gave me an encouraging word for Stranger Dude. But when my time ran out and my workout ended, I looked up and he was gone. That led to a mini-praise party in my mind because that was way easier than anticipated.

But as soon as I stepped off the elliptical and turned around, Stranger Dude was standing right in front of my face. The timing. The location. I almost did a holy hustle down the aisle, but instead I said, "Hey, bro."

He looked at me funny, probably trying to decide if we knew one another. I introduced myself, and he told me his name. It wasn't actually Stranger Dude.

"Listen, this may be weird," I said with a smile, "but I'm learning to hear God's voice, and I feel like I have something to share with you. Do you want to hear it?"

"Yes!" he said without hesitation.

I told him what I felt like God had given me, and more words quickly followed. It was like pulling tissues out of a tissue box, except with words—they just kept coming.

"I get the feeling you're going through a really hard time. It's almost like you're picking up all these broken pieces and trying to put everything back together, but it's actually hurting you. Does that make any sense?"

Before we get to the man's response, let's pause for a moment and look at what was happening. In previous chapters, we discussed how God can communicate through special circumstances as well as a still, small voice. God can give guidance and wisdom through visions, dreams, or a personal inner knowing. Holy Spirit can minister through you in various ways, including supernatural gifts.

About Revelatory Gifts

- ○ **Word of knowledge**—Holy Spirit reveals past or present supernatural details that you would not already know.

- ○ **Word of wisdom**—Holy Spirit reveals how to properly apply information to a particular situation.

- ○ **Prophetic word**—Holy Spirit reveals supernatural words that edify, encourage, and comfort other people. A great way to prophesy is to ask the Lord to give you a Bible verse or passage to share with someone.

God's reservoir of knowledge, wisdom, and encouragement is limitless. These gifts don't operate in your own strength, but through Holy Spirit. Sharing revelatory gifts requires maturity. You should always hold on to what is good and test all things (1 Thessalonians 5:19-21). This is not a way to make stuff up, judge people, or try to control a situation. Holy Spirit wants to minister through you to reveal His heart and vision for others. God gets the glory. We are to "follow the way of love and eagerly desire gifts of the Spirit, especially prophecy" (1 Corinthians 14:1 NIV).

For me, thoughts like the ones for Stranger Dude often come as a "knowing." It's as if a new and somewhat random thought pops into my mind, and it feels peaceful and clear, not chaotic. In the Bible, we see that God also speaks through visions, similar to daydreams, and through dreams at night.

Sometimes when I feel as if I have an encouraging word from the Lord that aligns with Scripture, I work through a few helpful, practical questions to decide how to proceed:

○ Have I seen any media or been in a conversation recently that would bring this seemingly random word to mind? If the answer is yes, I proceed with caution.

○ Does this glorify God?

○ Is this thought for me, for another person, or for the church?

○ What is the relationally appropriate way to proceed?

○ Does God want me to share this right now, save it for later, or just pray for that person?

○ How can I give God glory in this?

After I overanalyze all those questions, trusting Holy Spirit is continuing to provide a sensitivity to His voice, I move ahead or reassess. Sometimes I don't have time to review all those questions, and when that happens, I try to lead with courage.

FUN FACT

The Lord gave Ananias a vision that played an important role in Saul's conversion story (Acts 9:10). In the book of Acts, the gospel spread through revelatory dreams and visions.

———————————— ○ ————————————

Let's go back to the gym. I quickly ran through the checklist and gave Stranger Dude that encouraging word about picking up the broken pieces. Not wanting to force my agenda on him, and knowing it's important to create space for conversation, I asked him if it was making sense.

Blinking back tears, he nodded yes.

I felt as if we weren't quite finished. "Hold on to hope. God loves you—you are not alone, and He will help you through this time."

He responded, "I have multiple sclerosis, and my doctors don't know what to do with me. I feel like they all gave up and I'm all alone in this. It hurts, and I just don't know what to do. I started coming to the gym hoping it would help, but my body is deteriorating."

As we continued to talk about faith, the process of healing, church, and next steps for his journey, we both recognized how miraculous this moment was. We decided to go to the health director at the gym and told him this crazy story of our divine meetup. Shocked and awed by God, the director set him up for wellness coaching.

AS HOLY SPIRIT MINISTERS THROUGH YOU, HE MAY SHOW YOU THINGS THROUGH THE REVELATORY GIFTS. AS THIS HAPPENS, PEOPLE FEEL KNOWN, SEEN, VALUED, AND LOVED BY GOD.

God recognized Stranger Dude's desperate need for physical relief and responded with something even better—supernatural relief.

God has been revealing things to you since you became a Christian, and maybe you weren't even aware. That "fluke" when you decided to call a friend the day she was feeling down? Holy Spirit setup. That time when your thoughts got interrupted to pray for your son and you found out later it was right when he was having a hard time at school? Holy Spirit reveal. The time you felt compelled to chat up a stranger who ended up being a lifelong friend? God was speaking!

We need people like you who are aware of the way God moves and alert to His promptings. Holy Spirit wants to show even greater things to you so He can continue to minister to and through you. As He moves, people feel known, seen, and valued. The love of Jesus is revealed. Don't miss it!

SIMPLE PRAYER

Lord, lead us as we step out in greater risk to share Your love. Fear has no place here. May we bring You glory. Amen.

DAY 27 HEARING AID: CREATION

The goal of these hearing aids is to show you ways you can cultivate a lifestyle of power in God's presence. Today, take time to quiet yourself before the Lord and listen to His close whispers. Quiet the distractions and go outside to a peaceful spot in nature. Settle your mind on the Lord—you can do this with or without worship music. Prayerfully ask Holy Spirit to minister through you using the revelatory giftings.

JOURNAL PROMPT

Who is on your heart?

What did God reveal?

Now work through the six questions on page 164 and proceed however you feel God is leading.

After you finish this challenge, check it off on the contents page.

28

EMPOWERMENT

She stands at the end of the cliff, hoping to experience the joy of flying through the air and splashing into the deep waters of the lake. There's a rush of uncomfortable excitement as she looks over the edge. Her mind races with the what-ifs, screaming to her that she'll land on a hidden rock underneath the surface. Maybe she'd be the queen of all belly flops. As she looked at the vertical jump, she felt all the emotions that went along with stepping into this—the fear, possible pain, surrender, excitement, courage, victory. It's a moment of choice every cliff jumper has to make. She can take the plunge into the deep waters or turn around and safely retreat to flat ground, wondering what would have been. She has options. Then she hears a familiar voice she knows.

"I'm right here. Do you trust me?"

It was the voice of her father, and his arms were stretched open. They shared a rich history, and she knew his heart for her was good. She knew her dad wouldn't invite her into chaos. She knew the plans he had for her weren't to harm her but to give her hope. She was strengthened by his voice and realized she could trust the father she knows, even when the outcome was unknown.

So she jumped. The falling felt like time had paused, and her heart was beating in tempo to her screams. She was scared but secure. As she was empowered to surrender, the greater adventure unfolded.

The adventure in the Christian journey isn't about the landing, it's in the surrender. Your character isn't strengthened in the outcome, but in the confidence-building moments leading up to the jump.

> *Beloved, if God so loved us, we also ought to love one another. No one has ever seen God; if we love one another, God abides in us and his love is perfected in us. By this we know that we abide in him and he in us, because he has given us of his Spirit (1 John 4:11-13).*

God's love empowers action. We love because He first loved us (1 John 4:19). Your love *for* Him comes *from* Him. Love is not manipulative, serving to be loved, because you already are loved. God's love is freely given. His love rescued you and empowers you to love others.

God's presence brings miracles through willing cliff jumpers like you. Your love springs from His love. Your service flows from His love. When you feel led to pray with a stranger, God's love replaces the paralyzing fear that grips you. His love anoints you to bring good news to the poor. His love empowers the blind to see and the oppressed to be set free (Luke 4:18). If God gave a donkey the ability to speak truth, I'm pretty sure He can use you and me too.[12] You get to be a part of something that can be explained only by a God who loves.

GOD'S LOVE EMPOWERS ACTION.

Christianity is not limited to an hour on a Sunday. It's a lifestyle that God reveals to us and that burns in and through us with passion and action because of the love of Christ. You want revival to come into your home, job, school, church, and country? Have reverence for the love of God and understand that revival starts in your own heart. Revival starts in the heart of individuals—in your heart and in mine. As we stand on the edge of the cliff, we are empowered to understand the depths of the love of God. He changes our heart to trust, to repent, to surrender, to declare victory over darkness, to lead honorably, and to understand God as sovereign and good even through the what-ifs and unknowns.

What keeps us from fully taking the plunge into being fully available to God? *We do.* When we have been motionless, we need to be set in motion. We aren't created to stand frozen at the edge of the cliff, wondering where our gifts fit in or unsure how Holy Spirit operates through us. We are empowered to boldly love others just as Christ loves us. What if the solution was and will always simply be *Jesus*? Together let's commit to following Jesus and falling into His freely given love.

Every day you will have moments when you get to choose to be a cliff jumper. Will you hear the voice of a loving Father inviting you to leap into the deeper waters? May your response be empowered by His love.

SIMPLE PRAYER

Lord, may we have a deeper

revelation of Your love today!

Amen.

DAY 28 HEARING AID: BIBLE

Are you looking for a special way to encourage others? Try sharing a Bible verse. Pray for someone in your life to receive new momentum. Ask God to highlight something in the Bible that will confirm what He is doing in that person's life.

JOURNAL PROMPT

Who is Holy Spirit inviting you to encourage?

What Scripture passage could you share with this person?

After you take the leap and reach out to this person, journal about the experience.

29

ENCOURAGEMENT

Be encouraged to be an encourager. It's a spiritual art that everyone can learn. And mostly you learn by practicing it.

JILL BRISCOE

If you knew where a dirty and scuffed-up gold coin was buried on a beach, would you go dig it out? Of course you would…and please tell me you'd yell like a pirate as you shoveled through the sand to get that treasure. Even a hidden and neglected gold coin has great value.

When I teach my kids about biblical encouragement, I describe it as seeing people the way God does. We need to dig past what we see outwardly and focus on their inherent value. No matter how messy or damaged their lives may seem, they are infinitely valuable. We need to trust Holy Spirit to empower us to see the gold in people. ← *Even ourselves.*

> **One who prophesies strengthens others, encourages them, and comforts them (1 Corinthians 14:3 NLT).**

One of the ways Holy Spirit communicates through people is with the gift of prophecy. As He does, He reveals God's will for the present and sometimes for the future. Holy Spirit speaks through people to share divine encouragement

HOLY SPIRIT WANTS TO SPEAK THROUGH YOU TO BRING ENCOURAGEMENT AND LIFE THROUGHOUT YOUR SPHERE OF INFLUENCE.

about situations, ourselves, and others. As that happens, those who receive His encouragement are strengthened, gain direction, and feel seen by a loving God! Prophecy helps us see people the way God does.

I have seen the Lord give businesspeople specific next steps in their businesses. In the church, I have seen Holy Spirit confirm leadership changes and building moves, encouraging and strengthening the people's vision. I have seen God confirm individuals' calling, empowering them to serve others in creative ways.

Here are some practical reminders about how the prophetic gift operates:

○ Prophecy points to Jesus, just like all other manifestations of the Spirit (Revelation 19:10).

○ Prophecy never contradicts Scripture.

○ Prophecy strengthens, encourages, and comforts (1 Corinthians 14:3 NIV).

○ Prophecies should not be treated with contempt but should always be tested (1 Thessalonians 5:20-21 NIV).

○ We prophesy in part (1 Corinthians 13:9).

○ A prophecy is not a solution. Prophecy points us to the solution—Jesus.

○ We are accountable to share our words appropriately and live accordingly.

FUN FACT

The word "prophesies" comes from the Greek word *prophēteuō*—the act of revealing something that is hidden, disclosing the will of God, or foretelling the future.[12]

Receiving a Prophecy

The common caricature of prophets shows them standing on platforms, perhaps wearing a sandwich board, yelling doom and destruction all up in everyone's face. (They shouldn't.)

Or maybe someone announced (complete with "Thus says the Lord") that God wanted you to move to a third world country and raise baby elephants, but God never gave you a vision for any of that. When a prophetic word seems to come out of left field, remember that prophecy doesn't dictate your next steps; it confirms them. Prophecy can encourage us, but it doesn't replace our security in Christ. If you receive a potentially life-changing prophetic word, trust that Scripture, Holy Spirit, and your church leaders will help you know how to respond.

Giving a Prophecy

Let's not print business cards with our names and title: Prophet of All the Land. But what if… Could Holy Spirit actually use us in this way? After all, we are to "pursue love, and earnestly desire the spiritual gifts, especially that you may prophesy" (1 Corinthians 14:1). What would it look like if we began desiring divine encouragement for others and trusted that Holy Spirit wants to minister through us?

My friend Lauren and I had been invited to help out at our church's women's conference. Our responsibilities included giving announcements, leading in prayer, and closing the worship sessions.

During the final worship session, I asked the Lord what He wanted to focus on, and I felt like He said, "Encourage the legacy these women carry because of the hope they found in Me. It will transform generations to come." As those comforting words felt firm on my heart, I thought of Anna, my friend's daughter. I felt strongly that she was the one to pray over the younger generation.

I ran it by the women's pastor and Anna's mom. We quietly talked with Anna about it as women continued to worship. She felt nervous and afraid and didn't know what to say.

Here's the thing. Weeks earlier, God began orchestrating this moment. Another woman in the church began encouraging Anna to consider taking on leadership roles similar to this. Her parents, who are leaders in the church, had been talking with their kids about walking in obedience and not missing out on opportunities to serve.

With an uncomfortable yes, Anna jumped into this divinely orchestrated moment. This 13-year-old walked onto the stage in front of hundreds of older women. Holy Spirit poured out encouraging words as Anna spoke with God-confidence and anointing. Women felt God in her words, and some began weeping. Some of those who were present later commented that the experience was the most transformative moment of the conference. I'll never forget watching Anna prophesy.

The same Holy Spirit who indwells her also indwells you if you're a believer. He can fill your mouth just as He filled hers. Who knows? Maybe He's been positioning you for such a moment, just as He did with Anna. Whether you're on a stage, at your small group, or in a supermarket, be on the lookout for ways God orchestrates moments to strengthen, encourage, or comfort others. Simply see people the way God does, and then start talking.

SIMPLE PRAYER

Lord, equip and empower us to encourage others.

Amen.

DAY 29 HEARING AID: CIRCUMSTANCES

God is always speaking, but we often forget to listen! Every morning I try to share "morning motivations" with my family. I try to see them the way God does and encourage them accordingly. You can give someone a morning motivation by...

○ affirming their character traits (the fruit of the Spirit)

○ celebrating the ways God is moving *in* them to be more like Jesus

○ encouraging the ways God is moving *through* them to serve others

This is a great way to honor people in your life. You aren't glorifying them, but glorifying Jesus moving in and through them. And let me tell you, whenever my kids give me some morning motivations in return, it's a really special thing.

JOURNAL PROMPT

Who will you share a morning motivation with today?

What will you say?

How did they respond?

Don't forget to check off this hearing aid on the contents page after you've completed it.

30

TRANSFORMATION

The Holy Spirit never enters a man and lets him live like the world.
You can be sure of that.

A.W. TOZER

A group of women in my community are raving about a man in town who calls himself a medium and psychic. They're trying to find answers by communicating with the dead. Why are they doing that when they can freely communicate with the One who gives life? They are searching for an experience that will show them there's more to life than the one they see. Yet they are legitimizing an experience that is deeply deceptive—and paying $600 to do it!

As believers, we have an all-access pass to a holy and personal God who is intimately involved in our personal lives. If you've been completing these daily readings and hearing aid challenges to become more attuned to God's voice, then I'm confident Holy Spirit has been transforming you. As you meet people who are desperately searching for answers and changes in their lives, remember that Holy Spirit is empowering you to point them to the one who holds the solution—Jesus.

Transformation is a miraculous process through which God connects people to the power of the cross. We see a great biblical example of this in Peter's life. He was being held in jail in order to be persecuted. From the outside looking in, his situation seemed pretty grim. For days, Peter could have easily thought

God wasn't doing anything about his terrible circumstances.

But the church was praying. The night before a trial that would determine his fate, when most people would be wide awake with anxiety, Peter was sleeping soundly, bound in chains between two guards. He carried the peace of Christ into his horrible situation.

Then God did the miraculous. He transformed everything. He sent an angel who miraculously opened doors, caused prison chains to fall off, and escorted Peter out of jail as a free man. So what did Peter do? He immediately shared this testimony, and people were astonished and amazed as they heard about a God who does awesome things (Acts 12)!

> TRANSFORMATION IS A MIRACULOUS PROCESS THROUGH WHICH GOD CONNECTS PEOPLE TO THE POWER OF THE CROSS.

The same God who transformed Peter's captivity into freedom has also transformed the very things that kept you in chains. He can bring peace to moments of chaos and deliver you into far greater freedom. As we've seen so many times so far, Holy Spirit dwells in you and moves through believers like you. You've already seen what God can do—in fact, you've seen Him change your life. Let's affirm that the way God is moving right now is just as significant as the ways He's moved in the past. You are no longer enslaved by sin, but transformed into a Bible-believing, Christ-following woman or man of God. You weren't born into that freedom; Christ revealed Himself to you, and you are changed as a result. Revelation 12:11 says that we triumph through the blood of the Lamb and the word of our testimony. Christ can use your freedom story to help others connect with Him.

People are hungry for purpose. What would happen if the next time you tell someone, "I'll pray for you," you actually paused and asked if you could pray for that person right there in that moment? What if the next time a friend was struggling to find meaning and purpose in the mundane moments of motherhood, you shared an encouraging word from Scripture? What if the next time you sit across from your friend or family member over coffee, you shared the story of one of your transformative moments in Christ? You don't need to shove your Bible down anybody's throat or speak Christianeze or splash anointing oil on their head or have an altar call. Simply share what you believe Christ is doing and see where the convo goes from there. You can also take it a step further and ask them how they see God working in their life as well. Be led by the Spirit as you share. Just as God used Peter's jail testimony to point people to a miraculous God, He can and will use yours too.

SIMPLE PRAYER

Lord, transform our thoughts so they align with Yours. Transform our priorities so they match Yours. Transform our actions so they bring You glory. May we see the moments of transformation and share the testimony of Your victories, and may others come to know and celebrate You too!

Amen.

DAY 30 HEARING AID: WORSHIP

Spend time in worship today! Have your Bible nearby as you spend time in God's presence. Prayerfully ask Holy Spirit about the way you talk with unbelievers. Is anything keeping you from sharing about the power of the gospel?

- ○ fear
- ○ intimidation
- ○ lack of knowledge
- ○ don't make it a priority
- ○ don't care
- ○ [fill in the blank]

If talking about the transforming power of the gospel is difficult for you, consider this: Worship helps you focus on Christ. As you become aware of obstacles that may be keeping you from freely sharing about what God has done, trust that worship will awaken you to heaven's perspective.

JOURNAL PROMPT

How did your time of worship affect your thoughts and feelings?

Did you sense God speaking to you? If so, what was the message?

Did God reveal anything about Himself to you? If so, what was it?

31

HOW IS HOLY SPIRIT WORKING THROUGH YOU?

The gospel is moving forward as Holy Spirit operates through us in our homes, neighborhoods, churches, schools, and businesses. God is on the move around the world, and we're in on it! Our hearts are awakened to revival, and we come expectant for the miraculous. We're pushing aside the perfectly curated social media feeds and opting instead for honest, authentic communication. We're so done with canned Christian phrases that reflect our culture rather than Christ. We battle complacency in our faith. The watered-down gospel that keeps people feeling comfortable has no place here. We've learned to hear Holy Spirit in every season—when we hurt and when we're happy—knowing full well that God remains in both. Pain and joy can coexist. Even through the suffering, God is sovereign and good. We're walking in our giftings and gaining heaven's perspective in a deeper way. We're overflowing with possibility and God's promises and celebrating all God is doing!

Congrats for making it through act 3. Drop your accountability partner a note of celebration and encourage them as well!

        o *Did it!*   o *Nah, I'm lazy.*

Let's recap some key takeaways:

- ○ God's purpose releases His power and promises, creating new possibilities.
- ○ Obedience powered by Holy Spirit is a faith walk that trusts in a God who actually knows what He's talking about.
- ○ Holy Spirit fills you with joy and hope that others find contagious.
- ○ We can walk confidently with Holy Spirit's guidance.
- ○ When Holy Spirit moves freely in our lives and our churches, we experience miraculous unity.
- ○ As Holy Spirit ministers through you, He may reveal a Bible verse, an encouraging thought, or an insight in how to pray for another person.
- ○ God's love empowers action.
- ○ Holy Spirit wants to speak through you to bring encouragement and life throughout your sphere of influence.
- ○ Transformation is a miraculous process of God that He uses to connect people to the power of the cross.

You're commissioned to continue boldly stepping into all God has for you! You're learning how to hear God's voice and how He speaks to others. Regularly choosing to be still with Holy Spirit, study the Bible, and participate in church will provide a healthy faith foundation for you. The holy habit of resting rather than striving transforms you as you listen to God's voice. The daily moments of pressing into God's presence empower you to resist pressure from other forces. You are noticing God's work on the earth, and He's daring you to risk big as you continue to walk in your calling. You're hearing God's voice, doing His will, and loving others well.

OUR HEARTS ARE AWAKENED TO REVIVAL.

The world is saying, "Look at me!" but you're rising up and saying, "Look at Christ!" You are part of a generation that doesn't give to get but gives and remains unseen. You lead from love, and that shifts people's eyes to our Creator.

Declare victory over sin. Fight for social justice in communities that haven't changed for decades. Crave authenticity and vulnerability in a way that breaks the grip of inadequacy. Be a leader who follows Christ. ← *Be still. Get filled to overflowing.* Christ is using you to boldly speak, serve, and love. You've discovered Holy Spirit in your everyday life, and everything has changed. While there is still breath in our lungs, you're not done! God is on the move.

SIMPLE PRAYER

Holy Spirit, we celebrate all You've taught us

and empowered us to experience. Thank You for

moving mightily in so many ways. May we glorify

You all our days. Less of us, more of You, Lord.

Thank You for loving us.

Amen.

DAY 31 HEARING AID: FREESTYLE

To celebrate all your hard work in completing the hearing aids, go out for ice cream or to your favorite restaurant. Since we've learned that Holy Spirit is speaking through everyday situations, prayerfully ask Holy Spirit how He is moving through you. He may give you an encouraging word for your dinner companion, invite you to overflow with generosity and bless your server, or lead you to someone who is "at the right place at the right time." Trust that God is speaking, and take action as He leads.

JOURNAL PROMPT

How did it go? Whom did God lead you to? Describe your interaction.

What feelings did you experience along the way?

After you've written about your experience, talk with your accountability partner about it or share it online using the hashtag **#GettingToKnowGodsVoice**. After you do, check off this hearing aid on the contents page. If you missed any challenges, start working on those today. You're designed for this—continue the forward momentum in hearing God's voice in every area of your life!

SO YOU MISSED IT

"God told me I was going to be married by this November!" my single-and-ready-to-mingle friend said boldly as she ripped photos of wedding dresses out of magazines. Autumn ran right by, and we all wondered why this Jesus-loving woman wasn't running to the altar. Did she hear God correctly, or did she eat too much pizza the night before?

We've all been there. I know I have! You thought you heard God's direction for your life, but the whole thing turned into a big, confusing mess. Maybe you took a risk and trusted that God was using you to share empowering words, but you were actually riding the hot-mess express.

So you missed it. Now what?

O God is greater than your mistakes, and He gives grace. We all make mistakes that we can learn from. Are you extending grace to yourself too?

O Take appropriate responsibility. Do you need to apologize to anyone?

O Don't give up, but remain humble and be willing to change and grow. Is your security in Christ or your situation?

We're at the gym, building our spiritual muscles, remember? As you keep Christ in the center and read the Word, remain humble and navigate the gifts alongside healthy leaders. Remember, in your self-perceived failures, you are loved by a God greater than your mess-ups!

WHEN GOD IS SILENT
or at least it feels that way...

Open your Bible; God is speaking. As you become increasingly familiar with the Word, you'll recognize His voice. He'll speak as you read the Bible, and as you go about your day, He'll remind you of verses you read. He may even prompt you to share them with your friends.

If you're in a season when it feels as if God isn't speaking, try reviewing act 1, where we explore various ways He communicates with us. The Bible promises that as we draw near to God, He will draw near to us (James 4:8). Don't be rigid or legalistic about it; just maintain your passion and be intentional to show up. Surrender your agenda for His. Spend time outside and in worship, get to know the character of Jesus, read your Bible, connect with other Christians, and go to church (take notes during the sermon!). And remember, He is always there. God is always present. Holy Spirit dwells in you and moves through you. He doesn't always shout; He whispers because He's already close. He's speaking; position yourself to listen.

NOTES

Chapter 1: Introduction to Act 1
[1] Special thanks to my theological editor, Brayden Brookshier, for developing this thought.
[2] 1 Corinthians 3:16
[3] Romans 6 and 7

Chapter 5: Worship
[4] James 4:8
[5] 1 Samuel 16:14-23

Chapter 7: People
[6] 2 Peter 1:19-21; Proverbs 15:22

Chapter 8: Prayer
[7] Matthew 4:1-11
[8] Matthew 14:23
[9] "Silent and Solo: How Americans Pray," Barna, August 15, 2017, https://www.barna.com/research/silent-solo-americans-pray/.

Chapter 16: Isolation
[10] Hannah Schulze, "Loneliness: An Epidemic?" Science in the News, April 16, 2018, http://sitn.hms.harvard.edu/flash/2018/loneliness-an-epidemic/.
[11] Numbers 22:28

Chapter 29: Encouragement
[12] M.S. Robertson, "Divine Revelation," in Lexham Theological Wordbook, ed. D. Mangum, D.R. Brown, R. Klippenstein, and R. Hurst (Bellingham, WA: Lexham Press, 2014).

CLOSING CREDITS

God—thank You for changing everything for me on June 4, 2000. I'm still flabbergasted You positioned me for this project, and I have faith You'll carry these words as far as You see fit. **Matt**—you spent hours processing theological concepts with me as this book was being formed. Your leadership in our marriage and businesses brings greater freedom to our family! **Max and Zoey**—the way you serve, love, and are getting to know God encourages me. I'm so mama-bear proud of you. **Dad and Mom**—thank you for always being my biggest cheerleaders. **Brayden Brookshier**—thank you for being my theological editor and overanalyzing biblical passages at all hours of the day. Your love for the Word is contagious. **Gene Skinner**—team Rander could not have done this without your patience, kindness, and God-given gifts. I'm beyond thankful you carried this project over the finish line. **Steve Laube**—your wisdom and support spoke strength over me when I felt out of place. **Barb Sherrill**—thank you for letting God minister through your giftings daily. I'm honored to be a part of the Harvest House family! **To the rest of the Harvest House crew**, your creative ninja skills brought this book to life. **Anne Bean, LeAnn Foss, Olivia Richardson, and Amy Terry**—thank you for serving Freedom Creatives and being involved in the development process of this book. **The Servellos, Schillings, Langes, and Bellars**—thank you for your leadership in my life, your pastoral counsel, and your love for our family. Your obedience in building God's kingdom is far-reaching. **My church family (past and present), and Brynn Shamp, Michelle Cuthrell, Maria Trexler, Candace Payne, Mimi Majerus, Jeremy, and our ministry prayer team**—your prayers, support, ability to process through some Randle rambles, and deep theological debates are invaluable to me. Thank you for your friendship. And to you, **dear reader**—thank you for making yourself available to hear God's voice.

ABOUT THE AUTHOR

Jenny Randle is a nationally sought-after speaker, award-winning creative, faith-based podcaster, and author of *Courageous Creative*. She guides believers, creatives, and church leaders into a space of freedom in their personal lives, leadership, and church culture.

Jenny has served in ministry while working in the entertainment and creative industries for 15 years. In 2009 Jenny was recognized with one of the highest honors in the entertainment industry—an Emmy® Award.

Over the past decade, God has used her creative expertise, love of the gospel, and gift of encouragement to passionately communicate His kingdom to the heartbeat of our culture. She has taught at major leadership events and has preached at women's retreats, churches, and conferences nationally. Her topics range from biblical creativity to understanding the Holy Spirit. Jenny also speaks on leadership and professional development. She's been a rising voice in mentoring aspiring authors and creatives and has been featured in nationwide press and heard on top-ranked podcasts.

In early 2018, Jenny and her husband, Matt, formed Freedom Creatives Inc., a ministry organization dedicated to developing resources that merge profound gospel-centered truths with practical application. As she has communicated online or in person, God's message of hope, healing, and Holy Spirit revelation has helped thousands of people discover and live out their calling.

Jenny resides in Northern Florida with Matt and their two kids, Max and Zoey. They enjoy beach life and pray they'll continue to throw confetti-like praise in the air for all of their days.

For more information or to invite Jenny
to speak at your event, visit
jennyrandle.com

You've courageously learned to hear God's voice...
now stretch your God-given creativity as you do!

Courageous Creative is written for every wounded creative or procrastinating dreamer to empower them to discover the freedom to create again. This hands-on journey will give you the tools and encouragement you need to discover your God-given identity, cultivate your creativity, and express your thoughts.

"Courageous Creative is a near-perfect spark for out-of-the-box thinkers and creators—and for anyone looking for creative moments in dormant areas of everyday life."
CANDACE PAYNE —viral sensation, speaker,
and author of *You Belong, Laugh It Up, Defiant Joy,* **and** *Simple Joys*

For fun, creative challenges, and to learn more
about *Courageous Creative,* visit
jennyrandle.com